TRANS NATURE

BREAKING BINARIES
FOR INTEGRATED BEING

by Sue Hunt

Cover art & chapter ink by Persimmonstudios.com
Subtle Body Sketches by Becky-jane.com
Interior layout by Chriswilliamsdesign.co.uk
www.the-numinous.com

For my parents

Elle, a psychologist, artist, intuitive and empath.
Turner, a dreamer, serial entrepreneur, a master
of action and expansive thinker.

Both healers within their intergenerational inheritance and the
dissolvers of generational karma. Parenting with radical love, and
inclusivity. These pages originate from the seeds of change they
planted in their own lives and mine.

///

Respect for the teachings and their evolution.

I have been a student of Vedanta, Modern Yoga, and Buddhism for
more than half of my life. In this text Sanskrit and Gurmukhi are
both cited out of respect for the origin of the practices and cultural
traditions from which this profound wisdom originates.

CONTENTS

FOREWORD

When writing my first book, I was on a mission to codify a Consciousness Design Process.

Our communal language definitions are often built on binaries. We process the world in a rigid way, pitting what appears to be two opposites against each other, in an either/or way of seeing. In the years that led to me completing this project, I kept hearing and seeing suffering arise from this either/or language, and how it shapes thought, identity, and the evolution of consciousness in divisive and limiting ways.

Language and the sacred art of communication have the profound ability to shape how we perceive ourselves, one another, the world, and the Universe as we know it. In collective speech—a powerful consciousness organizing tool—expanded ways of communicating, and therefore being, exist beyond the binary spectrum of opposites. In developing Non-Binary Worldview, we see a new set of summational archetypes emerge.

At the same time, there is very little conversation, practice, and embodied integration around living a life of both/and, and the full exaltation of our mysteriously evolved complexity. It's as if we stand at an interesting juncture, where we know there is a different way forward, but within our Binary Worldview we can't imagine the consciousness structure that will take us there.

This is the journey of this text: A Consciousness Design Map towards summation, embodied transcendence, and clairsentience, or the ability to perceive states of consciousness and creative ways of being that exist beyond the binary. Through this, there emerges an integrated, interconnect-

1

ed being with access to expanded states of consciousness, exalted senses, and elevated capacity.

Each section is an evolutionary building block towards the embodied integration of Non-Binary Worldview, or an uncovering of your Transitory Nature. Give each section the time, love, and attention it deserves. I propose 30 days of personal practice and contemplative inquiry for each section. This Consciousness Design Process is the culmination of the last 15 years of practice and teaching, and, as I have done with my students, I suspect you will revisit many sections, practices, and realizations for years to come.

As a spiritual teacher, I am deeply invested in the path of personal empowerment and spiritual sovereignty. I desire this for every single being who picks up this book. It is not my goal therefore to have you "trust me"; self-transcendence requires one to deeply trust the empirical data that rises out of your own body/mind relationship without reference to or measurement by any outside metric. It is my goal therefore to build faculties of deep self-resonance within you, so that you are able to more deeply trust the sustainable path of your own contemplation, and allow others to do the same.

I like to imagine we're meeting in person. If we did, I would throw my arms around you for a huge loving embrace. I imagine it all the time. I picture someone thumbing through these pages on the train, asking themselves big questions about living a more easeful and abundant life, and why it seems so elusive at times. Another being pulls out this book at a coffee shop, sipping a latte as they consider the sacred vessel of their body and a more integrated gender expression. I see the audio book on someone's lock screen on their lunch break, as they think deeply about their personal purpose and its overarching implications in creating a more ethical society. Each of these beings is deep in what I see as an *identity restructuring process*. Each also senses the possibility to bring about change in the fabric of mainstream social structure through these shifting internal inquiries by fully integrating their Transitory Nature into their worldview and actions.

I came to this work myself through walking the path of both teacher and devoted student simultaneously. I too have had my dark nights of the soul, processing deep trauma, integrating realizations around heavy emotions, and modifying behavior through loving, potent, focused, clear meditative attention. Other worlds of being, dreaming, listening, and creating opened up due to the non-binary way of viewing the world that emerged as a result, and through learning to see my identity as a fluid, shapeshifting structure that carries both ME/WE within the limitless potential of the body/mind.

Part of my Dharma is to share this work as a catalyst, so that it might spark realization in others as they break their own binaries and embody a both/and approach to Reality.

You're next!

INTRODUCTION

If we examine the building blocks of our modern identities, we find that they often exist within the oppositional limitation of binaries: *success/failure, right/wrong, male/female, conservative/liberal, beautiful/unattractive*. Fit *in*, or you're *out*. These binaries are passed down through our family units, religious influence, political affiliations, traumatic experience, cultural conditioning, social structure, and language construction, creating what I call a "Binary Worldview." This is the idea that everything must be either one thing or the other. Binary Worldview is so ingrained in our contemporary psyches that it causes extreme personal suffering as we struggle to find our infinite potential within "this" or "that." In this struggle, a painful schism opens up between our lived truth and binary society's intellectual grooming and social pressures. Binary Worldview is entrenched to the extent that it is almost impossible to escape. Many of us have rebelled against our upbringings, institutional values, and mainstream prescriptive behavior, in an attempt to feel more like ourselves. But what often happens is that our rebellion simply forces us to the other end of the binary, where we find ourselves equally purposeless and boxed-in.

Binary Worldview is actually rooted in the strongest, most ancient psychological impulse of humanity, which is to avoid pain and to gravitate towards pleasure, a misperception around the cyclical process of life/death itself. This life/death, pain/pleasure binary takes us on many twists and turns in our lived experience. In thought, action, and speech, we cling to everyday comfort and familiarity, seeking a sense of perceived "safety" and continuity within repeated, recognizable versions of self.

But this in and of itself obfuscates the profound fluidity of our true nature. Why? Stagnant and outdated binaries barely scratch the surface of the limitless potential that is accessible through growing into the non-binary summational archetypes that arise out of our Transitory Nature. In shifting the perceptual architecture away from the "familiar," we become divining rods for the uniqueness of our purpose and its contribution to an interconnected social structure.

In my 15 years as a spiritual guide, I have been in contact with thousands of students. That means thousands of stories containing immense complexities of both suffering and realization, which often exist simultaneously. Whether coping with the inevitability of death, pulling back the layers of self-punishment, swimming upstream in corporate America, moving through anxiety and depression, or healing family trauma, the conflicted self-identity and personal misperception they grapple with can feel endless at times. And within all of these disparate stories, I have continually sensed and helped those living them to confront Binary Worldview, which turns out to be at the heart of so many violent conflicts within.

Binary Worldview seeks to create definable categories, labels, and boxes, diminishing cognitive and psychic abilities over the long term. It leaves us all feeling constricted and displaced in our own bodies. Shameful and fearful in our minds. Questioning ourselves based on others' perceptions, words, or judgments. We constantly feel the violent clash with institutional values, social pressures, and delusional cultural narratives that pit us against our own humanity.

And, make no mistake, this is the result of an imbalance in the power-hungry human consciousness, having been infiltrated by extractive colonialism and the need to control the masses over the centuries. When we commit to living beyond the binaries, we no longer struggle to "fit into" a worldview that is strategically designed around power and oppression. In opting out of this worldview, we naturally begin to shape the world around us from the inherent fluidity we were each born to embody.

The purpose of this book is to help you recognize where you have been trapped within the binaries, and, in doing so, to catalyze an integrated way of being that is a profound reflection of your Transitory Nature. This happens as we settle into a seat of deep integration that breaks through the many oppressive binaries through which we define ourselves. *The end-game? A life lived in service to our elevated human capacity: creative, regenerative, non-competitive, and based in systems of care not exclusion.*

Building a Non-Binary Worldview is about holding opposites on a continuum. Freeing ourselves from the reductive understanding of the pain/pleasure binary and the many separating consciousness structures that grow from this binary. Leaving limiting labels behind, and stepping out of the either/or mentality that perpetuates violence to self and others. The ability to do this originates from deep comprehension of the thoughts that limit us and their projection on the collective—something you will also be invited into with this text.

In the process of breaking your binaries and uncovering your own true nature, you will cultivate the emotional and psychic sensitivity to meet another being in the eye of their own storm, without becoming swept up in drama or losing the dynamic recognition of your own ego-structure (the term I use to indicate the profound depth of the ego's "scaffolding," and how our thoughts, choices, and perceptions don't just stem from a single place). You will sharpen your intuitive communication with self and others, and deepen your ability to understand the multi-faceted fractal nature of human experience, free of labels and judgment. Non-Binary Worldview allows each one of us to intimately know the many layers of our identity, creating a clean, energetic pathway to live creatively and purposefully.

This Non-Binary Worldview respects difference, holds opposites without conflict, and is endlessly regenerative in nature, expanding the resilience of your central nervous system to embody creative solutions, as well as to enact personal and social change. Meanwhile, the process of breaking our binaries requires mind training and steadfast contemplation. It opens us to many ego-deaths and evolved iterations of self-identity. Don't worry, we will get there together!

Engaging with this field guide is a collaborative project between you and me. As a deep feeler and intuitive thinker who is personally dedicated to living and communicating with engaged compassion on the daily, my mission with this text is to birth a nonviolent way of being that honors the fluid self-identity and pure creativity within us all. Together, with each sentence, we will strip away binaried, hierarchical, and inherently destructive thinking. Together, we will break from limited self-identifications that are obstructing radiant creativity and expressive joy. Along the way, my hope is that you will uncover your true "home" frequency, and the profound potential of its impact on the world.

BREAK YOUR BINARIES AND RECLAIM
YOUR SPIRITUAL AGENCY

Right/Wrong. Rich/Poor. Just/Unjust. Me/You. Sane/Insane.

At its core, the work of breaking the binaries is about delivering back to you full agency over your life by training the mind to see value beyond category and hierarchy. Binary Worldview strips us of our most potent human skills: intuition, creativity, and innovation. Instead of exploring and cultivating the full spectrum of human experience, and our ability to accept and ethically inhabit our true sense of self, the limited self-definitions of Binary Worldview diminish our full psychic capacity for elevated consciousness. When we see ourselves in binary terms, we outsource our power while in turn dimming the brilliance of others, because the binary itself is dulling our skills of nuanced discernment.

This leads to a host of societal problems. For example, our mental health model seeks to diagnose deficiency and disease, but can often negate an understanding of the complex set of personal needs that supports us in our thriving. Moreover, this model negates the power of working with, cultivating, and visioning societies and identities based on altered states of consciousness. From our current vantage point, I use the word "altered"; but in actuality, these transcendent, clairsentient states of consciousness are always available to all of us, and Non-Binary Worldview is the vehicle for accessing them.

Defining ourselves using the linguistic simplicity of binaries also often leads to spiritual bypassing and/or an existential crisis, both personally and communally. Within new age spiritual rhetoric and academic fields, we often hear terms like "wholeness," "transpersonal psychology," "humanistic approach," and "intersectionality," which attempt to speak to the fluidity of human consciousness. And yet, these fancy words often only reinforce an intellect/intuition binary, without laying the framework for embodied realization within our own hearts and body/minds.

So why are we so attached to the Binary Worldview?

Beneath our attempts to use this worldview to "make sense" of an innately numinous Universe, lies a potent, seductive force:

The Illusion of Choice
From spiritual and religious leaders to neuroscientists, we often hear that happiness, thriving, moving out of victimhood, and success are mind-states that we can and must choose, when in actuality they are often the by-product of doing the hard contemplative and embodied work of breaking out of Binary Worldview. If we strip away the many hierarchically violent, oppressive, misinterpreted, unconsciously accepted definitions of personal identity and mainstream archetypes, personal happiness, freedom, and fulfilment are inevitable! Yet, when we believe this is about making the "right choice"—defined as the choice that will lead to greater happiness, satisfaction, or pleasure—we are only seeing a small sliver of the full picture of what's actually available to us.

The illusion of choice exists in an either/or binary that actually strips us of our full personal agency.

We are currently witnessing massive social and political unrest, which is tremendous! The social constructs of race, class, gender, upward mobility, and politics are built on some of the most intractable binaries of all. Yet our current paradigms for healing, inclusion, and structural reorganiza- tion are failing us. Why? Without first dismantling Binary Worldview, we are dressing up the same violent issues of separation, oppression, and domination in different costumes.

For example, the notion of "equality" presents quite a conundrum inside a binaried worldview. Only an identity that is category-less perpetuates freedom: empathy for all points of view. This is not to strip each of us of our unique heritage, but it is a call for us to no longer weaponize our perceived differences against one other, causing yet more hierarchy. An identity marked by category always diminishes the vantage point of what it is NOT, thereby creating power hungry stratification that only seeks to reinforce the binary, and we all suffer. And all of this operates within the fundamental pain/pleasure binary, which seeks to make things "better," without questioning the assumptions, identifications, and agendas which inform the Binary Worldview that lurks beneath.

Human existence is not just about "doing better," "fighting the good fight," "finding balance," or "becoming whole." When we commit to breaking out of Binary Worldview, we stop chasing "wholeness" and instead cultivate fluidity of identity, which is fertile ground for a revolutionized vision for personal and communal expansion. This process, as outlined in this text, dramatically restructures our vision of self, our connected surrounding reality, and our ethical impact on breaking down violent mainstream binaried consciousness.

Instead of seeking wholeness (which implies an inherent brokeness), Non-Binary Worldview believes that *human consciousness is organized in limitless fractal patterns. By expanding our view of ourselves and the world, the game of choice expands to include limitless possibilities for all.*

On the other side of this/that lies a future that holds symbiotic respect for our selves, each other, our global population, and earth. Within the pages of this guide, we will cultivate the capacity to go from this/that to BOTH/AND/MANY/NEITHER.

Now, we are experiencing true Spiritual Agency, holding in our sights a vision of a summational non-binary archetype of consciousness.

When we stop wasting precious energy both operating within and rebelling against Binary Worldview, we open ourselves to energetic sovereignty. To cultivate Spiritual Agency we need to examine where, how, and when we unjustly give away our power. In this process, we free ourselves to focus on the higher octaves of human consciousness, such as intuition, psychic knowing, and compassionate and heart-centered equanimity. This Spiritual Agency lays the groundwork for "protest living," a way of being that originates from a deeply transformative frequency, rather than operating within existing societal binaries that leave us trapped and fighting against one another.

The contemplative work of this book is designed to help you codify a design for life that has not yet been invented, because it defies labels and categories, and exists beyond the illusion of binaried choice. When practiced with vigor, the examination and reorganization of identity is inherent in this process and cultivates a self-sovereignty that in turn supports interdependent community wellness, while being preventative against violence towards self and others.

HOW TO USE THIS GUIDE:
ACTUALIZING NON-BINARY WORLDVIEW

Each chapter follows a similar structure, and addresses one of the nine binaries (of hundreds) that I have identified as structural glitches within our constructed worldview. As such, this text outlines a nine-month Consciousness Design Process, with each section outlining 30 days of practice. Uncovering your Transitory Nature requires deep personal inquiry, daily practice, and integrated realizations. Each section contains a road map to realizing the non-binary archetype in your conscious awareness.

As we meet each binary, you will also meet yourself in narratives drawn from my students' lives, which encompass the stories and experiences that personify Binary Worldview. I want you to see yourself and your personal struggle reflected back in these pages. Then, we will dissect and debunk the cultural myths that have been built on each binary, excavating the commonplace language and cultural assumptions that keep this binary thinking hidden in both our self-identities and social institutions.

Moving into a space of personal reflection, contemplative writing, and practices will then encourage a deep dive into your own suffering as caused by these binary identifications. Through writing reflections, emotional purging exercises, and embodiment rituals, you will train yourself to recognize the "aha moments" of breaking the binaries as they occur.

At this point, you will begin to see your worldview shift dramatically. Dissecting, learning from, and evolving your own lived experience of Binary Worldview is integral to our work together. Remember, I am here with all of my own compassionate humanness to support you on this path of egoic destruction and divine radiance. Finally, after you have taken the time to experience embodied realizations about your own binaried misperceptions, I will lay out the new path forward.

Each chapter is also accompanied by a Subtle Body Practice that will take several forms throughout the text: from more traditional meditation and attention training techniques, to embodiment practices that encourage integration and revelation. Each practice is intended to be done for at least 30 consecutive days, in conjunction with that chapter's Personal Inquiry Practice and Breaking the Binary exercises.

Neural rewiring, auric field reprogramming, and the reorganizing of the meta-dialogue (meta-dialogue being a term for the many intra and inter-personal messages that create our specific perspectives and, when investigated, can help us understand when we separate from our true nature) happen with velocity and potency alongside committed *sadhana*, or personal practice. You might hear the ego voice making up many excuses to skip these daily practices. Remember: the practice itself is the very tool needed to compassionately confront that voice that fixates on self-sabotage, and prevents self-identity expansion. Resist the urge to skip this section, and stay committed to this practice alongside your contemplative work; we don't shift our worldview or the worldview of others by thinking alone. True transformational shifts come from deep internal knowing that often transcends language and is felt in the fabric of our beings.

In praxis, this means it will take approximately nine months to work through this text, dismantling one binary per month. However, the internal restructuring that is beginning to take shape is designed to be an ongoing process. Try to stay committed throughout, and, if confusion sets in, remember to seek guidance first and foremost in the practice itself, and in your own self-resonance and embodied empirical datum.

THE 9 BINARIES

Before you get started, let's take a closer look at which binaries we will be working with, and why.

THE FIRST BINARY
Private/Public: Symbiotic Ethics

Each of us has experienced the struggle of trying to reconcile our Public faces with our Private lives. This struggle to unify the pieces of our fractured identities often leads to codependent behavior in both realms, as we seek validation and acceptance through Public recognition, and then use our Private lives to unload the excess emotional pain that comes from not showing our true selves. In this chapter, we'll dismantle this Private/Public binary, investigating the many masks we adopt as we navigate the world, and working to uncover and integrate the identities beneath, in order to lay the groundwork for interdependent relationships and ethical behavior.

THE SECOND BINARY
Sick/Well: Transitory Nature

In Binary Worldview, Well-ness is envisioned as the end goal of healing—a static state of healthiness, happiness, and high-functioning in the world. At the other end of the binary, Sick-ness, which results in death, is to be avoided at all costs. As we struggle to avoid our inevitable mortality, we engage in shiny cover-ups to keep us appearing "Well" that actually prevent us from being present for our full human experience. When we commit to breaking this binary by accepting and celebrating the Transitory Nature of all things, we are able to embrace the natural life/death cycles in our lives, honor our limited time on earth, and fully inhabit our ever-changing bodies and spirits.

THE THIRD BINARY
Masculine/Feminine: Body as Vehicle

The moment we come into this world, we are spiritually and psycholog-

cissexism · belief or assumption that cis people's gender identities, expressions + embodiments are more natural + legitamate than those of other people.

cis / derived from cisgender, someone who identifies with gender assigned @ birth

sexism / system of oppression, rooted in superiority over others.

+ disadvantage for transgender + nonbinary people

ically projected upon in a gendered way. In Binary Worldview, the Masculine gets equated with a picture of strong, rational progress, and the Feminine with a soft, intuitive wildness. Even when we commit to seeing Masculine and Feminine as concepts that co-exist, we place ourselves within these poles and end up perpetuating cissexism, heteropatriarchal oppression, and limited notions of self-expression and identity that keep us from investigating who we really are. In this chapter, we'll interrogate this either/or categorization of our bodies and identities, and open to transcending the binary by transforming our bodies into fluid, creative vehicles for societal change.

THE FOURTH BINARY

Lack/Abundance: Pranic Economy

Within the Lack/Abundance Binary Worldview, our value is equated with a narrow, capitalist concept of productivity and cash flow. We are left constantly feeling the Lack of "less than," and scrambling to fill up on so-called Abundance without dealing with the hollow places within us that are devoid of lasting worthiness. In this chapter, we will identify areas of Lack in our lives that keep us trapped in cycles of empty consumerism, and redefine "capital" within the context of a sustainable energy exchange that honors and replenishes our intrinsic resources, and shifts how we make, spend, and share our wealth.

THE FIFTH BINARY

Hustle/Flow: Elevated Capacity

Our current binary view of work keeps us on the endless hamster wheel of Hustle's goal-driven "more, more, more" mentality, where Flow is either obtained by learning to master the relentless rhythm of continual motion, or is positioned as the elusive reward that comes at the end of all this Hustle exhaustion. In this chapter, we'll interrogate society's addiction to busyness, overproduction, and martyrdom—redefining what success looks like to us, reconnecting to our vibrant creativity and innate imagination, and swapping self-care hacks for a sustainable flowstate that values our self-sovereign, intuitive capacity to navigate our lives.

14

THE SIXTH BINARY
Root/Crown: Integrated Being

Home to our basic human needs for safety, emotional regulation, and desire fulfillment, our "Root" is seen as the ground from which we can grow towards a receptive, intuitive "Crown." In Root/Crown Binary Worldview, many of us struggle with Root Deprivation issues—operating from fear-based scarcity mentality that leads us to either obsess over and get mired in dealing with earthly matters like money, sex, and power, or to avoid them entirely as we race to achieve spiritual success by attaching to an intellectualized and dissociative version of Crown energy. In this chapter, we'll challenge our perceptions about "low" versus "high" spiritual work, and fortify our capacity to truly receive both the earthly Root stuff of life, and the actionless receptivity of an intuitive Crown.

THE SEVENTH BINARY
Attachment/Aversion: The Middle Path

Each of us is motivated by a complex network of "likes" and "dislikes," and when we start to cling to these Attachments and Aversions, we often end up believing in an unchangeable version of "the way we are" and "the way things are." These beliefs unconsciously affect our relationships with others, leading to entrenched patterns borne from unexamined preferences and deep fears. In this chapter, we'll examine what we cling to, what we disavow, and where we get stuck on a painful autopilot that keeps us from honestly engaging our ever-changing selves, relationships, and lives. Then, we'll forge a Middle Path that softens our attachment to control and the illusion of a "stable" self, building compassion for the many points of view and possibilities that surround us.

THE EIGHTH BINARY
Self-Will/Destiny: Karma + Dharma

We all long to connect with our soul-purpose, harnessing our particular skill set in service of a larger whole. But when we get trapped in the Self-Will/Destiny binary, we end up either struggling to "Self-Will" our lives into being, exhausting ourselves by fighting against what cannot be changed and missing out on a sense of universal collaboration; or we give it all up to Destiny, passively getting tossed about by chance without ever really connecting to our personal passions and potency. In this chapter, we'll explore the karmic imprints that we each carry, healing from judgment and shame around our limitations and patterning. We'll then learn to use our acceptance and understanding of our unique makeup to uncover the sustainable service of our Dharma mission, activating our creative life force in co-creation with the Universe.

THE NINTH BINARY

Past/Future: Clairsentience

The stickiest, most stubborn binary of them all, Past/Future shapes our deepest beliefs about who we've been, who we are, and who we can become. Caught up in the limitations of linear time's concept of progress, and a desire to "locate" ourselves within a continuous identity that moves from the Past and towards the Future, we suppress our ability to access the timeless intelligence that exists in any given moment. In this chapter, we'll grapple with the "Associative Architecture" that keeps us replaying rigid notions of the Past that limit our Future and short-circuit our ability to create true change. This will leave us ready to tap into the limitlessness possibilities that are always present.

Be extremely gentle with yourself when engaging with the reflective inquiries and Subtle Body Practices I will ask you to explore throughout. I often remind my students that integration happens through experiences of pleasure and safety, and so in order to cultivate resilience and self-trust, we must leave time for non-striving, non-doing, and non-pushing within our daily flow. The meditative work in this text builds in intensity as we approach boundless intimacy with our own self-identities. Before we begin, here are some pro-tips to remember when we are undoing deep programming:

1) Be less social and reevaluate the amount of energy you expend outward.
2) Choose social environments you can safely learn from and reflect upon.
3) ASK FOR HELP! It would be so transformative to do the work in

each chapter with a friend, a partner, a sibling, or a family member for processing and reflection purposes.

4) There is no rush. It is far more advantageous to work at a slow, sustainable pace, keeping in mind that your tolerance for change and evolution will ebb and flow with the demands of life.

I will also be defining and using lots of new, non-binary language. I will be introducing concepts that you may have never heard of before, to which there is a quick reference guide on my website at www.transitory-nature.com for further study and personal inquiry. I invite you to be thorough in incorporating this new language in both your identity and your lived experience. And, as I always say to my close students: *I am here if you need me.* Humility and adaptability are key pillars on this path. Saying "I don't know," "I need help," or "I need support" is an extremely powerful step in Breaking your Binaries, uncovering your Transitory Nature, and coming closer to Integrated Being. Thank you for allowing me to walk alongside you on this path.

I.
ROOTED IN
REALITY

THE FIRST BINARY
PRIVATE/PUBLIC: SYMBIOTIC ETHICS

From a young age, deep feeling and an expansive inner landscape were a part of my identity. Yet I often felt as though what I was experiencing in the "privacy" of my own consciousness was not acceptable to or welcomed by others. Growing up, I spent a lot of time "watching," "noticing," and "sensing" what I saw as inconsistencies between what people said and what they did. I eventually decided that holding my tongue was not an option, and I began forgoing social niceties in favor of speaking my truth.

While I was an extremely happy and motivated child, I didn't have many friends my age—not because I was rude, but because I was always questioning and challenging authority. I was sometimes labeled as a disobedient troublemaker, and by my extended Southern family's child/superior power dynamics, I definitely did not exhibit "good" behavior.

Typical modes of punishment also did not leave negative imprints on my psyche, pressurize me to change my behavior, or suppress my inner rebel and willingness to speak up. I didn't experience much shame in front of my peers when I was called out or publicly punished. I knew who I was and what I wanted. And I was very, very vocal about this, taking every opportunity I could to explain what I thought and what I needed.

By age eight, I would leave class peacefully, halfway through a lesson, packing my backpack and calling my mother to come pick me up, explaining to her that I didn't need to repeat a lesson plan that I already understood, and that I was therefore done with school that day. While I wasn't a loud or obnoxious child or teen, I simply saw the world through the lens of pure reason. I didn't see the point of going against my own internal logic to "fit in."

To this day, I remain "quiet" in public, eschewing some of the usual social niceties. When I meet new friends, I often warn them: *Hey, if you see me on the street and I don't wave back, please know I'm not being rude. I am just in my own world.* But while I was, and am, deeply introverted and sensitive, and feel more secure in Private, I also have a lot of fire and revolution within me. Working for a cause larger than my identity is hard-wired into my being. Because of this drive, I have always pushed myself into the Public realm, taking a seat on student council, and joining community service clubs as a kid. Motivated by moral causes, I'd find myself speaking up for my younger sister when she was bullied, standing up to boys in Middle School who were mean to girls about their looks, and organizing school-wide revolts and protests against unjust disciplinary action.

Using my voice in Public in this way has been my own inner-consciousness raising work. I've constantly weighed the potential energetic fallout of both "options": choosing to stay silent or choosing to speak my truth. Behaving with intensity in Public as a female-bodied person and spiritual teacher has often created push-back from anyone perceived to be "higher up" in the power structure, as well as policing from peers when my actions have challenged their own ideas about "proper" Public identity. Facing both behind-the-scenes cutdowns and more outward judgments from others, I've worked hard to learn composure when speaking out in Public.

But this level of mental gymnastics can take its toll. Stepping into the role of teacher required me to be in "Public" every single day of the week. Again, I was a part of the spiritual community I aligned myself with, while also slightly alienated from it. I often felt like I was living a duplicitous double life, moving between my resilient Public persona and my deeply sensitive Private self. This double life feeling was further exacerbated by the perceived power structure of teacher/student, and student expectations about how a teacher was "supposed to behave," which often bound me to an external code of comportment that didn't really fit.

On a typical night arriving home from a day teaching, I would walk in the front door, my body's layer of protection falling off. No need to stand up straight or present in a way that was acceptable now. Standing in the kitchen over the counter, eating leftovers, alone at last, I'd unclasp my bra so my breast tissue could breathe and my rib cage could relax.

Or after an event, the fake smile would disappear from my face the moment I left. On the drive home, I would replay my discomfort about the endless handshakes, hugs, smiles, dismissals, or microaggressions before my rational mind would butt in to say: *But it was a "success." People really enjoyed it. It was a great turn out.*

For years, I struggled in this space. I felt like I had to present a re-touched, magazine version of myself to the world because that's what would make me successful, helping me attract students and make money. Inside, it ate me alive knowing I was selling a watered-down version of myself—the part that never "rocked the boat"—allowing others to inter-face with me and leave unchanged, because the messy truths remained unsaid. If only I were willing to bring these Private truths into the Public sphere, my work and my social mission would have more impact.

We all know the feeling in the pit of our stomachs when we compromise the totality of ourselves to fit in:

If I told my friends the truth, would they still accept me?
I am speaking out on this issue, but am I living it behind the scenes?
I love doing this, but will others think it's weird?

Within the Private/Public binary, we often define the Public by our jobs and co-workers, our creative works in the world, our extended families, friendship groups, and the communities we frequent. At the Private end of the binary lies everything we do behind closed doors, within the nucleus of our intimate relationships, and even the Private thoughts we keep to ourselves in our heads.

The Public end of the binary relies on an oppressive doctrine of "manners" and "politically correct behavior" developed by a racist, classist, sexist society. Meanwhile, socially accepted standards of Public behavior shift from place to place, requiring us to develop and maintain a keen sense of tactfulness, and a willingness to compromise our personal ethics given the social context. As we move between different environments, we immediately begin to adjust our own presence to fit within this unspoken psychosocial oppression. This is so subtle and instinctive that it quickly shapes our neuro-linguistic impression of self and other.

Over time, this Public end of the binary is where we look for acceptance, safety, and appreciation, diminishing inner connection for a dopamine hit of outside validation. The rise of social media has only exacerbated this. And as we come to rely on this validation of our Public persona, we become codependent on the gaze and the approval of others, fearing that showing our whole, unedited, Private self will lead to rejection.

When oppressive codes of Public behavior keep us disconnected from Private inner truths, this causes cognitive dissonance—the sense that we are "living a lie." The result? Many of us then expect our Private spaces to hold the totality of all that is not deemed palatable for Public consumption. This may include our suffering, our anger, our confusion—anything we perceive may be a "burden" to others in Public space or that challenges binary worldview ideas about political correctness. Now, our inner world becomes a space to unconsciously dump our challenging emotions.

And the more we separate our Private/Public selves, the more we sever our Private intentions from our Public actions. People cannot rely on us to show up consistently and clearly. We slip into bypassing mode, skimming over the messy job of creating real, grounded ethical change—both in ourselves and in the world. We give up Spiritual Agency over our healing process and disconnect from any comprehensive ethical action.

We can see this disconnect any time we "point the finger" at the collective:

I want to run my business more ethically, but I have to keep up with corporate standards

Ethical content doesn't get likes; I have to give people what they want

The mainstream is ignorant and judgmental so why bother trying to reach them?

I am not a part of the problem—that's just how the system is

If you are only showing up in Public as an edited version of yourself, humanity suffers, as the unchecked, unethical, politically-correct systems continue to go unchallenged. We are not fully available to others, and they are not available to us. There are "holes" in the whole—and people keep falling through the gaps! Taken to the extreme, this binary can lead to the cultural epidemic of giving away self-agency and responsibility by relinquishing our power to others, as we refuse to accept the Public consequences and responsibility of living ethically, while remaining addicted to victimhood in our Private life. *brings / perfect for the circumstance*

In contrast, breaking the Private/Public binary asks us to discover and hone our own "Symbiotic Ethical Code"—a code for living that honors our unique, subjective experience and core values from the vantage point of dynamic interdependence. Following this code means committing to doing the authentic personal work in "Private" so we can stop projecting our inner turmoil onto the "Public," bringing us closer to our fullest expression, our truth. And through this process we realize that we are inherently connected. We see that: *honoring my fullest expression through action, thought, and speech, honors your fullest expression.*

With this interdependent worldview front and center, and less energy going towards upholding a constructed Public presence, we start to recognize the many ways we might have used our Public lives to bypass cultivating a Private moral code and to sanction unethical behavior behind closed doors. There's no longer anywhere to hide from our own hypocrisy, spiritual bypassing is no longer possible, and we have more energy available for stepping into our Spiritual Agency and living an ethical life.

This work begins with simple, powerful questions:

Am I the same person in Public as I am within the perceived protection of my Private life?

How can I cultivate an authentic inner dialogue with the many sides of myself?

How can I hold myself accountable for sharing the same person in Private and in Public?

Once I started asking myself these questions, shit changed, and it changed for real. I closed businesses and reopened new ones with more ethically organized structures and less commercialization. I walked away from the Public persona hundreds of students had come to expect of me. I left the city behind and decided to live closer to earth. This was not without fallout, as people whom I'd formerly been codependently connected with—as we had come to rely on playing certain "roles" for one another—often railed against my choices.

In Private/Public binary worldview, behaving "appropriately" in Public and dumping unprocessed emotions in Private results in codependency at both ends. At the Public end, we become dependent on constant external feedback to constitute the truth of who we are; and in Private, we then expect those close to us to be able to hold all of the messy emotional fallout from not sharing our full selves in the Public realm. In the following sections, we will find where you hide in codependent behaviors at both ends of the Private/Public binary, dig into the micro of your Private self, and examine the imprint of your Public persona in the world. Then, we will lay the philosophical and metaphysical framework for a new kind of interconnected and interdependent humanity, as you formulate your own understanding of a Symbiotic Ethical Code that marries both your Public and your Private self in service of evolution.

THE MYTHS OF PRIVATE/PUBLIC

The Public end of the binary reduces complex situations to simple statements that are recognizable, sellable, and replaceable. These publicly-upheld platitudes often squash subjective experience, multidimensional levels of feeling, and intersectional identities into the oppressive boxes that create the very groundwork of all binary thinking, keeping us tied to an either/or, us/them mentality.

We often support and reuse these "platitudes" unconsciously, before we do our own Private morality checks, failing to investigate the implications of these Public messages and how they are actually divergent from living an ethical life. And this shields many of us from doing the inner heavy lifting required to align our Private beliefs with our Public roles.

As you will see, these Public "myths" actually uphold a binary worldview, and must be dismantled as we break through to a place of interdependent acceptance. When we buy into them wholesale, leaving them unexamined, we diminish our critical thinking faculties, bypass the personal work of cultivating personal morality and a more comprehensive worldview, and prevent the evolution of language that contributes to equality and structural change. Let's look at the specific myths that uphold and maintain the binary of Private/Public.

The Oneness Myth
We are all one
We are all love
We all hurt the same

When I read these words, I initially giggle and think "We are ONE? Why would I want your issues, your problems, and your judgments? Please don't assume you know my struggles, or project yours onto me!" If we really believed we were all one, it would also be impossible for us to witness any kind of harm being done to another being, and our spiritual practices would have far more traction in the realms of social justice, equal rights, and the abolition of oppressive institutional power.

So why isn't this the case?

Because this platitude of "oneness" is directly borne out of the codependent Private/Public binary. By claiming that we're all the "same" on the inside, our messy, subjective humanness is driven into codependent Private spaces where we "dump" the parts of ourselves that aren't or can't be acknowledged in Public. This process bypasses any real ethical engagement with what we and others need as individuals.

This notion of "oneness" also waters down the more complex yogic and Buddhist teachings of true interdependence, which spring from the

Misses the concept of ALL KNOWING Spiritual connection

29

understanding that all of existence is neutral or "empty," but that *context* can express to the observer where and how this neutrality is distorted by unclear perception. Neutrality holds all opposites within it: light/dark, up/down, Private/Public. Yet if we want to live beyond these binaries, we have to first explore how they express themselves within our personal context. If the goal is a truly ethical interdependence, this means we can't just jump to utopian ideas about "oneness" without first looking at our own biases and the fractured identities that are borne of the Private/Public binary itself.

Of course we are bound by the energetic substratum—the experience of humanness itself. But we must also consider that, as individuals, it is the context of lives and identities that makes us unique. Saying that "we are all one" both diminishes another person's unique pain and skill set, and denies the individual complexity of our personal healing journeys. When we attend to our specific, Private context, and our personal inner work, we actually increase the possibility of interconnection to all of humanity, and more ethical action and equality in the Public sphere.

The Vulnerability Myth

On the Public end of the binary, we deem "being vulnerable" and "feeling uncomfortable" as signs that we are getting it "right" and doing the "real" work. Social capital gets built around the idea of being "unapologetically me."

You scroll through your social media feed and see posts that state: *#nofilter #nomake-up. Here are my inner thoughts and personal stuff. I am about to get real and vulnerable.*

Self-help and wellness blogs claim: *In order to do the real work, we need to be willing to sit with the discomfort*

We see a lot of privileged women, in particular, acting as if "being vulnerable" is the way out of suffering, or that being willing to have "uncomfortable" conversations is the end goal of consciousness-raising endeavors. Mega celebrities have built massive platforms off these very ideas. Within the Private/Public binary, this teaching implies that when we show our "shortcomings" to others (from behind the relative safety of our phones), the reward waiting for us at the end is ultimate acceptance of self. But when we publicly assert how vulnerable we are being and how uncomfortable this makes us, we are actually playing into the codependent Public end of the binary: seeking validation for being "real" rather than doing the unseen, inner work of ego deconstruction through our Private processing mechanisms, and reclaiming our Spiritual Agency in the process.

If we really want to evolve beyond this surface level acceptance of self, and move towards more acceptance and understanding of others, we must realize that feelings of discomfort are an ongoing byproduct of contemplative living. In Private, the inner dialogue might sound like: *What if I get judged by others? What if I am wrong? What if I am insensitive in my delivery?* When you are integrating your genuine Private self with the expectations of the Public sphere, of course these things are going to happen! And when they do, we take responsibility and say: *I didn't know. I am sorry. Thank you for correcting me. I will learn more and make a change.*

Our binary worldview celebration of vulnerability is a stop-gap solution for the discomfort we inevitably feel when there is friction between who we are in Private and how we want to be perceived in Public. Instead of using our vulnerability and willingness to get uncomfortable as signs that we're doing the "real spiritual work," our sustained effort must lie in interrogating which of our perceptions are causing us to be different in Public and in Private in the first place. In our Personal Inquiry section, we'll start to gather intel on these perceptions, asking big questions about how we behave differently in different social contexts.

The Fronting Myth

There are many ways that mainstream calls to "action" ask for us to maintain and defend a Public image that exacerbates this binary. When we respond to these calls, we spend our limited energy "saving face" at the expense of the deep transformative work that actually lets us be of service. To get closer to interdependence, we must commit to honoring our difference by dropping these Public "maintenance" strategies and accepting the consequences.

Lipsitory [sin]ce 1991

The Call: *Put your game face on*
The subtext: In order to get through this, I am going to have to pretend in Public to be something that I am not in Private.

We put on our "game face" as we seek to protect ourselves from a challenging situation by strengthening a self-image that the Public binary perceives as "strong." This strategy takes us further from an integrated and ethical identity. When we put on one "face," and reject other parts of ourselves, the places we are hiding become painfully clear.

The New Response: *Take off ALL faces!*
Instead, look at the root of the issues you are confronted with from outside of your own identity and personal discomfort, examining others' points of view with openness.

Ask yourself: *How can I step out of my own identity (not just put another one on) and answer the dynamic demands of this situation without disrespecting the other point of view or forgetting to honor my own needs?*

The Call: *Put on your "big girl" or "big boy" pants*
The subtext: I am going to have to go against my own free will here, and answer the dynamic demands of this situation with a Public performance of maturity. I will have to deny my Private needs, will, or wants to get this done, or make it happen. Or... *find the courage you need to take on this challenge*

The New Response: Take OFF the pants!
Rather than putting on a fake "grown-up" persona, how can you tactfully dismantle the ways in which you have played small within an oppressive system, examining when you've allowed yourself to become a pawn rather than a conscious agent of change?

Ask yourself: *What am I being required to sacrifice and why? How can I respect my own needs while also responding to what's happening? What would the mature and self-honoring action be?*

The Call: *Just get over it*

The subtext: In order to maintain my dignity in Public, I will have to table my Private feelings about what has transpired.

To keep it "together" in Public, we get caught in a linear time trap, believing that "moving on" is a solution in and of itself, while ignoring the emotions that swirl within our Private lives.

The New Response: Deal with it NOW, or it's going to come up again!

If I buy into the idea that "moving on" is a solution in and of itself, while ignoring the emotions that swirl within, I will continue to expend energy indefinitely on "hiding" this issue in my Private life. When I tire of this, it will inevitably arise again.

Ask yourself: *What part of my inner self can I dialogue with about this issue? How can I shift from managing my Public responses to actually dealing with issues on a Private level?*

All we are doing when we submit to keeping up appearances is wasting our precious life energy holding up the walls of egoic self-protection. As we turn away from all of the behaviors that ask us to "front," we free up energy for the *real* real work of breaking down power dynamics and reintegrating fractured identities. Let's go deeper into this by exploring where this divergence between our Public and Private selves shows up. Then, we'll be ready to build an interdependent life that ethically aligns our Private selves with our Public actions.

PERSONAL INQUIRY PRACTICE: IDENTIFY YOUR PUBLIC MASKS

Symbiosis
Barriers between You and Me
Thin in Reality

Thick in the mind construction of
Self/Other

Permeable
A bleeding together
A sharing of all this earth
Has to offer
Paradoxically woven

Dynamic Ethics
In the personal spaces
Hidden places
Harmonious Synergy
A through-line inside out

The contemplative work of breaking this binary stares right into the heart of what I call our Embodied Identity Divergence: how our unconscious beliefs about "correct" behavior result in the creation of the many Public masks we adopt in different situations—through our bodies, thoughts, and actions. And how these masks diverge from our truest, Private selves and prevent us from acting ethically in the world.

When students sign up for my year-long contemplative program, I ask them to stop attending public asana classes. While many of us choose to participate in Public healing spaces, and there is certainly value to these settings, there is also a performative aspect that promotes codependency, as our practice becomes entwined with the need to "get it right" in order to gain acceptance. To challenge this, for 365 days, I ask my students to examine themselves in the spaces they deem "Private." Eventually, these discoveries help them to transcend the Private/Public binary as they learn to adjust their Public behavior to encompass the new realms of Private inner knowledge they have explored. Your shifting posture and your breath pattern always tell the truth, and identifying the difference between how you hold yourself in Public and in Private is the key to understanding how this binary becomes embodied—hidden in plain sight.

Follow this guide of reflections and prompts to uncover where the Private/Public binary manifests in your behavior:

1) *Over the course of a few weeks, develop a bird's eye view of yourself—meaning literally use your witness ability to watch yourself from the ceiling in the following kinds of scenarios.* Notice how you hold yourself at a party, or standing at a crowded event. Check in with your chest, your arm motions, the effort it takes to uphold acceptable body language in public. Also check in with your breath pattern: does it feel relaxed or forced?

2) *Check in with how you hold your posture in several diverse Public environments: a family gathering, a business meeting, and a friend hang out.* How do you use your body to communicate, to fit in, and to shield your own needs so that you can remain a part of the group? Note the differences and inconsistencies in your overall "energy" from Public place to Public place.

3) *When you are all alone, how does your posture soften when it does not have to hold up political correctness?* Watch this closely! Learn from this personal teaching of how you adapt in Private.

What did you notice about how you hold and occupy your body in Private and in Public? How can you begin to integrate some of the softer points of *self-awareness* you uncovered in Private into your Public life? What does it feel like to bring the *self-consciousness* of your Public persona into your Private spaces? Play with this, and notice how energy runs through your body differently in Public and in Private, and how even small tweaks can start to affect how you perceive yourself and take up space.

Your Private/Public Venn Diagram
Each one of us will have a unique Private/Public "Venn diagram" that reveals the sides of ourselves we keep in the closet, and the personal work we need to do to understand why. Start by making a list of what you deem as acceptable Public behavior and a list of what you deem as acceptable Pri-

vate behavior, taking note of the shared behaviors that appear in both lists.

Ask yourself the following questions about your Public behavior:

1) *Why do I behave like this in Public? How do I hope I will be judged?*
Write out several scenarios and the perceived consequences.

2) *What societal standards say this behavior is "correct" for Public spaces?* Do I
ethically want to uphold those societal standards? Examine any "politically correct" behavior—who is it helping and who is it hurting?
Outline several scenarios in your personal and professional life.

3) *What Public behaviors help me maintain my power or standing? What ethical compromises did I have to make to keep this power dynamic alive?* Write
out several scenarios and the power complexities in as much detail
as possible, picking situations that feel sticky and really examining
the sharp edges of misperception.

Now ask yourself the following questions about your Private behavior:

1) *What voices in your head do you keep private? How do these voices encourage codependent behavior in the Private realm?* Write out their tone, their
sound, and their enticing verbiage. Outline the emotion attached to
the voices that you hide from Public scrutiny.

2) *What Private behaviors help me maintain equilibrium? Can I own those,
instead of hiding them?* Make note of these, not to "teach" others but
to remind yourself of your own agency. Make these visible in your
immediate relationships so they can support your actions towards
equilibrium.

3) *When I feel challenged or uncomfortable in Private, what codependent coping mechanisms have I developed to avoid responsibility for my own internal
state?* Notice passive aggressive behaviors, instances of pointing out

others' faults, or over-focusing on others' emotional needs at the expense of your own.

In addition, scrutinize what you would "never say" in Public, and where you make excuses in your Private life because you feel like no one is watching. The behaviors, language, and embodied practices we reserve for "only Public" or "only Private" are huge red flags, and show us where we are attempting to fit in, save face, and uphold personas, perpetuating false projections in the Public sphere.

Now examine how you embody the Private/Public binary in your relationships.

The parts of ourselves we reserve for Private space with self, partner, or close friends can reveal where we enter the codependent Private end of the binary. This is not to say that you can't "vent" every once and awhile, but remain aware that this venting is often part of your consciousness attempting to work through misperceptions of the Public. Relying on this outlet constantly for personal processing stunts the development of emotional literacy skills that can be honed by you and you alone.

Ask yourself:
1) *When, where, and with whom can you catch moments of "emotional dumping"—unloading on others before you have taken the time to contemplate and work through at least a partial piece of an emotional scenario alone?* No judgment if the answer is "I am not sure," or even if this is the first time you are taking on an inquiry of this nature within the intimacy of your private relationships.

2) *Begin to outline and reflect on the context of these relationship moments.* This inquiry provides a new and objective lens to begin to realize when and where you unconsciously might be exhibiting codependency. Noticing these moments in and of themselves starts to make room for more emotional literacy in your Private sphere.

While continually asking yourself about the reflective lines of inquiry above, one of the most profound Private practices can be to STOP ALL GOSSIP. Even if it's just you and your best friend sitting around the dinner table, gossip is simply an attempt to protect our own egoic projections. In committing to quitting this, we learn to stop pinning judgment, dislike, hatred, or blame onto others, and to take responsibility instead for our own responses and reactions to certain behaviors.

Identifying, interrupting, and working to dismantle all our binary-driven Private and Public behaviors will help us develop a fluidity between social spaces without compromising personal agency or morality, and move towards a Symbiotic Ethical Code that honors interdependence and challenges oppressive political correctness.

BREAKING THE BINARY:
YOUR SYMBIOTIC ETHICAL CODE

The above sections have revealed how the Private/Public binary creates asymmetry in our lives, perpetuating hierarchical power dynamics, codependent behavioral loops, and a misaligned sense of self. You have seen how, in Private/Public binary worldview, we often initiate from a place of defensive protection, hiding parts we deem "unacceptable" and performing behaviors we think are "right." We talk about "the collective," nodding our heads about our shared "humanity," while feeling threatened by any actual differences.

By contrast, Symbiotic Ethics asks us to move from codependent emotional bypassing to the realization of an interdependent understanding—which rests in our ability to hold, question, and integrate many points of view simultaneously, and to allow any perceived differences to unite rather than threaten us. We can build this ethical behavioral model by exploring and developing three key principles:

Spiritual Agency
Unique Context
Interdependent Consciousness

When we dig into these principles, our understanding of self, other, and the interconnections between the two EXPANDS dramatically!

Spiritual Agency

In binary worldview, the "collective" is commonly intellectualized as a homogenous blob that exists outside of ourselves. Unconsciously, we often "other" this collective, claiming that "it's not about me, it's about the collective," and thus absolving ourselves of personal responsibility to one another in the interconnected web of life

To break the Private/Public binary, we must redefine the collective as:

A BLANK SCREEN!

Each individual projects our Private beliefs onto this Public blank screen. When we position the collective in this way, we start to take personal responsibility for our projections, rather than placing the problem outside of us. Once we vow to uphold this interconnected worldview through speech and action, it becomes impossible for us to uphold a harmful status-quo.

Say this to yourself:
I am personally responsible for my projections
I am personally responsible for the ripple effect of my projections
I see the inherent global benefit of not "othering" the world's problems as separate from me

Unique Context

In binary worldview, we often equate interconnection with "sameness." We distort our self-identity to "fit in" to a discernible category, searching for a reflection we have been conditioned to recognize, and forfeiting our personal agency in the process, as we turn the inner radio dial on our unique context to match the frequency of what we perceive to be acceptable.

By contrast, Symbiotic Ethics asks us to remember that interconnection does not mean sameness, and that our authenticity arises precisely from our unique context.

When you catch yourself nodding along with a "popular" sentiment, ask yourself:

In order to agree or disagree, seeking recognition in that reflection, what are you denying about your own unique context?

Notice the dopamine hit that is produced when your ego feels accepted as one of the "cool" ones or "right" ones as you seek that version of yourself in the gaze of another. Catch this frequently in your body/mind. Consciousness in human form currently has approximately 7.5 billion expressions! If you are actually clear with your own identity, chances are you won't see a clear reflection of YOU anywhere. The ego-structure wants hard and fast definitions of what "I am," but the interconnectedness needed in order to break the binary and build a Symbiotic Ethical Code actually relies on honoring our subjective realities—the causes and conditions that are unique to each expression of consciousness. Start with the following exercises and give these questions and reflections room to breathe, noticing when you seek yourself in collective reflections and forfeit your authenticity in the process:

1) *Examine your motivations, intentions, and emotional turmoil.* Our projections tend to follow us no matter the perceived circumstance. Outline any persistent discrepancies between your Private and Public behavior that cause emotional turmoil, picking three that tend to show up everywhere.

2) *Commit to interrupting the ego-structure's futile attempts to seek "sameness."* Write out the places you feel the "most accepted." Then imagine another human who would feel just the opposite in this situation; give them your full attention, and attempt to hold these opposite

responses side by side—no need to convert, teach, or change one another.

Interdependent Consciousness

Once we examine where we seek sameness, looking for Public reflections of our Private selves in order to prove our very existence, we begin to understand that true interdependent consciousness is not achieved through agreed upon ideas but through acknowledging our inherent differences. This begins with us. Interdependent consciousness is built from first honoring our personal context, keeping our Spiritual Agency intact, and not stealing another person's inner work from them.

Commit to this credo:

TAKE EVERYTHING PERSONALLY
and
TAKE NOTHING PERSONALLY

Take everything personally:

I know I am a distorted reflection of consciousness being projected onto the blank screen.
Can I fully scrutinize my own wounds, and know my skills/weaknesses in order to understand how I am projecting onto the collective blank screen?

Take nothing personally:

I know the other is a distorted reflection of consciousness being reflected back to me.
What do I need to excavate from this distortion to better know myself?

Taking all of our own actions and thoughts very personally and running them through the gauntlet of contemplation allows us to be discerning about what we choose to project onto the blank screen of collective consciousness. And taking nothing personally allows us to recognize that every other human is going through the exact same process in their own unique way.

As each of us claims responsibility for our projections onto the blank screen, a symphony of collective difference is created. Now, higher octaves of human consciousness—compassion, empathy, and equanimity—can emerge through a trained central nervous system that takes responsibility and becomes accountable each time it diverges from interdependent ethical action.

SUBTLE BODY PRACTICE

Reclined Meditation for Subtle Symbiosis

This month-long practice is key to understanding the body/mind as an interconnected field of awareness: the body, the mind, the aura, and consciousness itself as a cohesive energy field. Because the body/mind receives different stimuli in the many spaces we occupy in our waking lives, focusing on this interconnected field of awareness is especially important for understanding and dismantling the Public/Private binary. Understanding our reactionary response to stimuli and processes of perception within a particular space is key to seeing the conditioning we carry from place to place. In this weighted *śavāsana*—lying down in a supine position—we will control the stimuli, creating a petri dish in which to observe the body/mind and consciousness.

This practice is strategically simple, and focuses on the embodied sense of what it means to feel stability inside the body/mind. The state of contemplation, which we will reference many times in this text, is one of holding all sorts of stimuli and perceptions simultaneously without always rushing to find the "right," "safe," "programmed," or "predictable" answer. Within the boundaries of our own skin, we practice feeling at ease in the space of nothingness.

Posture

There is no mental or physical cue in this posture. Simply set it up with care, and make sure you are comfortable—prepare as if you could lie here for 20 minutes plus.

Prop the back of the skull with a blanket or a pillow. As pictured below, please start with a 25lb weight. No need to make it fancy—use anything heavy that sits with ease at the top of the femur bone closer to the hip crease, and further away from the knee joint so as to not disturb the joint. The backs of the knees can be propped with pillows or blankets to prevent discomfort. Arms rest alongside the body and the chest is free to accept the gift of the breath pattern.

As you become more adept at quickly dropping into states of relaxation within the body/mind, your cervical spine and facial structure will receive much-needed rest. When I teach this in open public workshops, I often say, *wear the skin of the face like an egoless mask.* Take deep advantage of being alone with no need to engage with any social structure, or have any automatically programmed responses in the facial muscles due to the movement of the mind.

This time in relaxation is skillfully teaching you what it's like to swim in your own energetic sea. *What do I feel like? What is my resting state? How do I discern what is me, and what is someone else?* The first step in answering these important questions is understanding how you feel with yourself, by yourself, and observing yourself, with very little stimuli.

Timing

Set your timer for 20 minutes daily, and methodically practice relaxation, down regulation, and recognition of your own baseline frequency. Any time of the day works, just make the time for it. Multiple times a day is heavenly, seeing as our moods and energy levels shift over the course of the day.

THE SECOND BINARY
SICK/WELL : TRANSITORY NATURE

When I lived in New York City years ago (and what feels like lifetimes ago!), I worked for a high-profile philanthropic non-profit that focused on bringing integrative health modalities to cancer patients. I started as an intern, and as the program grew I took several positions out in the field— in diverse clinical and home settings—working with cancer patients who were receiving radiation and chemotherapy. During this time in my life, I thought hospice work was the path for me. And these in-home extended stays were eye-opening: informing my notions of sensitive, trauma-based care on a physical, emotional, and spiritual level.

At one point, I was asked to perform in-home integrative therapy visits for the mother of a dear friend of the organization's founder. Of course I said yes, eager to show up with my A-game considering the personal nature of the request. The patient, Deb, had been diagnosed with stage four lymphoma, and the family wanted to address the side-effects of the chemotherapy in a holistic manner. I was asked to be present for chemo treatments, and act as her patient advocate, transport, and integrative therapist. When I think about these visits, one vivid scene comes to me.

When I arrived at Deb's on that hot summer's day, her daughter Mary's cigarette was emitting thick smoke that seeped in from the porch through the open upstairs window. Exhausted and nauseated, lying on the bed, Deb didn't notice. All she wanted was for me to talk her through a meditation while I reiki'ed her feet.

Later, at a typical family meeting to discuss care for Deb, all four of her children exhibited layers of emotional intensity and complexity. I sensed both their guilt for outsourcing their mother's care to me and their gratitude for this care. The siblings debated schedules for "checking in on mom," and aggressively compared Google calendars—"but my kids, my dog, my job." The family was used to communicating with yelling and forceful language. Though disappointed with her children's intensity and lack of understanding for her needs, Deb's compassionate soul knew that they too were trying to cope with this change. She listened with a worn smile on her face. I stepped in to say, "Okay, let's let Deb rest." With the room quiet, Deb turned her head across the pillow to say, "Let's do that meditation—can we? It's quiet now."

In this moment I sensed her grappling with letting go of her old "high functioning, loves to be needed" mother role. There was no option; she could not pretend anymore—she didn't have the energy. She had been forced to step down from the caretaker role, and surrender instead to being cared for, asking for help from me to sort through the unnecessary "noise" to create space for her much-needed rest.

Moments like these were my great teachers in my early 20s. Here I was with all of my "wellness tools"—hundreds of meditation techniques, essential oils, healthy foods, breathwork, and more. But when it really came down to it, the deepest moments of realization stemmed from this truth:

I am going to die. How do I feel about it? How does everyone around me feel about it? Why am I worrying about everyone else? Death is staring me down; it is time to be present for it.

In the grand scheme of how we think about "health," while Deb was the "Sick" one, her children, at the other end of the binary, were "Well." They existed as part of productive, functioning families with lots of kids, high paying jobs, nannies, and able bodies to go about life as they pleased. Yet as they stood over their mother's bed, another story was present: crippling anxiety, immature coping mechanisms, emotional incompetence, and a high level of stress in response to the inevitable truth of their mother's passing.

The Sick/Well binary presents the idea that Well-ness is a state to be obtained—resulting in a high-functioning way of being in the world. And at the other end of the binary, death—the perceived eventual outcome of "Sick-ness"—is to be avoided at all costs. "Healing" becomes a goal in and of itself, and we end up working so hard to appear Well that we hide from our mortality, creating debilitating responses to avoid the reality of our expiration date.

What does "Well" look like in this binary? Picture this:

The alarm goes off. She rolls out of bed and puts on the coffee pot. She scarfs a protein bar, pops a cocktail of SSRIs and anti-anxiety meds, and then out the door for another busy, super-productive day. Day-in and day-out, no time to confront and contemplate her doubts, fears, and trauma residue that lie underneath. And the loop plays on—overbooked, no time for herself, deep sadness, popping pills to tamp it down and feel "okay." And repeat.

His posture is strong and guarded. Holding a straight face the whole time as his boss yells at him. Fighting back the memories of childhood beatings. Back to his desk to work harder for that bonus, and then he aggressively beats up his own body later in the gym. All for what? To prove to himself that he is "Well" by successfully dragging his strong body through this cycle over and over again.

When we chase the Well end of the binary, we go to destructive lengths to "hold it together" and "function" in the world. Well becomes "normal" and Sick, in turn, becomes a deviation. We keep the Sick parts of us hidden away, and we hide perceptions of our own sickness within the private spaces of our beings. In turn, this split keeps us from ever really learning the skills to properly address our underlying emotional, physical, and mental states.

The entire Sick/Well binary is built on the belief that human beings are inherently "broken" and must seek to "fix" whatever prevents them from participating properly in society. This binary is strongly connected to both capitalism—and its notions of linear improvement and progress—and a particular interpretation of Judeo-Christian teachings about repentance. These narratives creep into every aspect of our lives and self-identities. When we buy into the identity of "brokenness" we become hypercritical and perfectionistic, seeking to "better" the parts we see as "defective." Without realizing it, we begin to hide our total selves, reducing our truthful access to self-intimacy, along with our capacity for closeness with and empathy for others.

Medication, surgery, and even the drugstore makeup aisle and booming anti-aging market, all lead us to believe that with enough "work," we can remedy our brokenness and restore ourselves to perfect "health." Our ego-structures jump on board with statements like: "The treatments will kick in and I'll feel better soon;" "When my meds are over, I'll be happy;" and "Once this cellulite is gone, I will feel fully confident." Even the process of "letting go" in our current self-help, self-improvement vernacular reaffirms this deep attachment to the Sick/Well binary, as we scramble to release painful parts of ourselves and our stories in order to finally, one day, be "healed" and "Well."

How do we break this binaried cycle? The answer lies in embracing our Transitory Nature. This process asks us to first confront, contemplate, and accept the truth of our own mortality and the death cycles that permeate all of our existence. When we commit to this practice, we can stop running from and masking what we deem as "Sick-ness" (which is seen as bringing us closer to death) and begin living from a respectful and integrated place that honors our limited time on earth.

In the following sections, we will uproot assumptions about our brokenness that fuel the Sick/Well binary, examining where this self-improvement narrative lives within us and where we chase visions of Wellness that keep us from grappling with the realities of our lives. Along the way, we will come face-to-face with our Transitory Nature, meeting and accepting both the ephemeral and the eternal transitions we call "life."

THE MYTHS OF SICK/WELL

The Mind Over Body Myth

Binary worldview thrives on a separation and hierarchy between the body and the mind, and we see this established in our lives from a young age. From kindergarten, "good behavior" that gets rewarded often stems from maintaining a quiet, passive, and obedient body. As teenagers, we learn that acne, period cramps, and suicidal thoughts are "bad" and can be treated with a pill.

As such, our view of health is built upon a divide-and-conquer model that equates being healthy with getting the body "in line" so we can show up to serve at the altar of scientific intellectual society. We come to see the body as "less than," or somehow primitive, beating it into obedience as we fight the flux of its Transitory Nature. Before we know it, we're swimming in a sea of big pharma, Western medicine, industrialized food systems, and systemic disease—never having learned to develop the interpersonal, emotional, and psychic skills required to acknowledge and tend to the ever-changing needs of body/mind being.

Meanwhile, bodily symptoms aren't just an expression of "sickness." They are messengers explaining the many layers of consciousness that seek transformation, realignment, and deep processing. When we reduce ourselves to our symptoms, disease, or diagnosis, we compartmentalize ourselves, disregarding our full humanness. We even see this within some "embodiment" based somatic healing spaces, which often state that "trauma" is "stored in the body." But while it's true that past traumas leave imprints in the body, these imprints are not just limited by the flesh or what appears to be the confines of our individual body; imprints are stored in our auric fields and in the electromagnetic frequency of our entire body/mind. When we say that traumas are stored in the body alone, we contribute to the Sick/Well binary's limited, linear understanding of broken and healed, positioning emotional responses to trauma as "fixable" if only we are able to "extract" them from the body.

In my own work, I have often received requests to help students advocate for themselves medically. And beneath their desires to go off psychiatric medication or hormonal birth control, the through-line is clear: a desire to move beyond the mind over body hierarchy, and towards developing trust in their capacity to read integrated internal messages and take action based on this intimate personal knowing.

When we interrogate the myth of mind over body, we start seeing our-selves as a set of cohesive systems upon systems, and we understand that transformation happens on many levels simultaneously. Every time you read the word body/mind in this book, know that it means both—there is no separation, and no binary, here!

The Healing As Wholeness Myth

Let's clear this up once and for all: YOU ARE NEVER BROKEN. Much of the self-help rhetoric we hear preaches that healing equals wholeness. Beneath this language is a worldview subconsciously rooted in the Sick/Well binary of broken/fixed. And many of us unknowingly approach our body/mind from this vantage point.

You are healed when you can share your story out loud and it doesn't make you cry

You are healed when you are no longer triggered

You are healed when the same toxic situation doesn't come around again

In these scenarios, we see an underlying belief that no longer being "trig-gered" means one is "healing," and therefore moving towards Well-ness. But friction on our paths is not always something to deem as "negative" or in need of repair. Instead, friction can signify an ego-structure that is actually restructuring with less attachment—not seeking to obliterate our triggers, but building more objective resilience when we experience them. Instead of "I need to do more healing because I am still getting triggered by that situation," we shift towards "Intense situations arise, and I have a handle on how I choose to respond."

Yogic and Buddhist worldview teaches a radically different approach to understanding the intrinsically connected, subtle layers of the human experience. Within this non-binary worldview, we do not enter this world from a place of "brokenness" but from a place of past circumstances. We have come back to earth not to be "made whole," but to work out these karmic imprints. As such, we each enter the world with a specific energet-

We heal the trigger that "I" unstayed

54

ic shape, frequency, and structure. If we get lost searching for perceived "missing parts," we have deeply neglected our unique structure and its innate gifts. Instead of searching for "wholeness," what if we knew our own tendencies so well that we could honor how and where each of our puzzle pieces fits? This awareness would allow us to honor our Transitory Nature, and actually support one another in our individual paths.

The body/mind is built to self-regulate, rejuvenate, and recycle itself. It is often our own healing agenda that misinterprets and obstructs the surrender to this flux. When we try to micromanage the shit out of our healing process, we end up with self-will fatigue. "Healing" becomes the iron fist of control in disguise. This might sound radical, but there is no such thing as linear "healing," "getting better" or "becoming whole"— there is simply a dynamic flux that is you! When we start to detach from a static end goal of "healed and whole," we actually become more empowered to look at how particular causes and conditions arise in our lives and, in turn, are better able to cultivate the causes and conditions that create change that's in alignment for us, because our vision and our actions are sending the same messages.

Surrendering to the flux gives us access to personal discernment. Can you already feel how this starts to reduce attachment to personal drama, diagnoses, and definitions of self?

The Pain Myth
Pain. Trauma. Stress.

Within the Sick/Well binary, pain, trauma, and stress are seen as things to overcome and wounds to heal, and are associated with experiences we deem to be less desirable than "happiness" or "balance." Less pain, less stress, and less trauma are equated with moving towards Well-ness. Within this binary worldview, the power of pain is often dismissed, and most of us run from it, even within our spiritual language. I get countless questions about how to "do" spiritual practice when one is sick, or dealing with chronic pain or severe illness. And my general response is, "Well, practice that you are sick! Honor your illness and do not abuse yourself with a sadhana because your fabricated thoughts around 'wellness' cannot accept the reality of what your body/mind is experiencing."

A deep internal study of pain, trauma, and stress, is what gives rise to wisdom and resilience. Pain has the ability to immediately shift our perspective, our definition of self, and our understanding of a situation or circumstance. Rather than something to fear, it is something to respect! I am not suggesting that we masochistically seek to enjoy pain; I am suggesting that instead of running from it and privileging choices to avoid it, we give it our unbiased attention.

We can start by cultivating discernment around the following distinctions:

Self-Indulgent Pain v. Transformative Pain
Painful experiences that tighten the feedback loop of our addiction to self-diminishment or definitive outcomes, versus painful experiences that cause deep internal self-reflection and build inner clarity.

Ask yourself:
When faced with physical discomfort or mental anguish, does my mind leap to predict more pain and victimhood in the future? Or do I see discomfort as an opportunity to learn a new skill set or expand my self-definition?

Self-Created Stress v. Growth Stress
Stress that is created in our systems by projecting our own fears and misperceptions onto a person or situation, versus intensity that can actually be tolerated by the central nervous system and is asking our consciousness to uplevel.

Ask Yourself:
Do I often "upregulate" disproportionately given a situation at hand? For example, "getting huffy" before anything has happened, or engaging in constant cycles of complaint or a doomsday mentality. Stress that causes growth, on the other hand, sounds and feels like extreme discomfort, but with a sense of self-mastery and attentive focus.

Trauma Stagnation v. Integrated Trauma

Trauma Stagnation is when we define our future self by past trauma that we re-live on repeat, while Integrated Trauma is knowing when that past trauma loop has been triggered in our inner landscape and choosing how to respond.

Ask Yourself:

Do I find myself constantly recognizing "triggers," but feeling powerless to intercept them? This is a clear indicator that you have an intellectual handle on past pain— that you know your "shit"—but that growth has stagnated. Integration arises from behavioral change: changing the social, personal, and inner causes and conditions the moment we see that past trauma loop about to play out yet again.

When we don't distinguish between these states and simply say that "pain is bad, and discomfort is something to avoid," we are actually limiting our most potent life growth catalyst: PAIN, which I often refer to instead as "upregulation" in the system, to keep things more objective.

As we're inundated with instant gratification stimuli, ideas and images of what "happy and healthy" look like, and a myriad of quick fixes to deal with our discomfort, it takes tremendous resilience for us to do the inner work of building our personal spectrums around discomfort. Before we can break the Sick/Well binary and develop a lived expression of Transitory Nature, we must give our pain the utmost respect. In our Personal Inquiry Practice, we will examine the root fear that underlies why we view pain as "bad," and how this hijacks our well-intentioned attempts to "heal." Rooted in this deep self-inquiry, you will begin to retrain your central nervous system to be wired for resilience and objectivity around perceived discomfort, or Sick-ness, in your life.

PERSONAL INQUIRY PRACTICE:
YOUR LIFE FORCE CONTRACT

A life force contract
From me to me

My time, it's finite
My body/mind
Meant to dissolve into nothingness

Stepping into this fear
It's freeing
Love big, fall hard, sob for hours
In pain and joy
Collapsing into one another

A small soft creature
A speck, a nobody
A universe in myself
A somebody
No matter, trace the through line

Seeking approval
Squanders life force
Don't desire? Don't do it
Holding Truth?
Make it heard. Risk it all.

Meant to dissolve into nothingness
My body/mind
My time, it's finite
From me to me
A life force contract

Answer the questions below with extreme honesty. Take your time while reading this Life Force Statement to yourself. Read it daily. Allow a new-found voice within to respond with care over the course of your 30-day contemplation of the Sick/Well binary.

1) *What sicknesses and illnesses scare you the most? Have you seen any in your*

bloodline that have been very hard for you to deal with? Write this out in detail and be descriptive—feel your own pain and fear beneath these visions of and confrontations with the Sick end of the binary.

2) *Do you think of your own death often? Has your ego-structure conjured up a story around death? Or are you very dismissive of this reality, and have a hard time even thinking about it?* Note which end of this spectrum you are on. From there, write out three scenarios that feel like acceptable deaths for you. Note the time, place, and details of the setting and circumstances; your ability to be present in this writing is key to future integration. *Interesting* —

3) *Have you dealt with loss in your life? If so, please spell out all of the positive and negative ways you confronted this loss.* Spell out all of the mature and avoidant ways you dealt with loss in your inner and outer landscape.

4) *Expand the definition of death beyond the physical loss of body, to include expiration dates on situations, relationships, apartments, jobs, etc., and ex- amine how you coped during these different death cycles in your life.* There will most likely be multiple answers to this question.

While this chapter's Personal Inquiry section may seem "short" compared to some of the others, please do not underestimate the profound nature of the above writing prompts. It may take you several visits to fully flesh-out the complex relationship you have with death. Breaking our overactive obsession with the Sick/Well binary lies in our ability to accept our Tran- sitory Nature with spiritual maturity. Allow these self-inquiries above to unfold alongside the work of the Breaking the Binary section below, and please return to these contemplations several times this month, answering the questions again once you have more intel from your life explorations.

BREAKING THE BINARY: TRANSITORY NATURE

Within the Sick/Well binary, we adopt identities around a picture-perfect idea of "healed," seeking to become the strong one, the caretaker, the "Well" one. And in the process, we often end up suppressing our honest reactions to the flux of our lives, and therefore short-circuiting our ability to actually cope with the natural life/death cycles of all things.

At one end of this "healing" binary we become self-obsessed, as we engage in frantic individualized efforts to unearth the damage done by personal dramas—often at the expense of acknowledging our shared humanness. At the other end of the spectrum, we adopt the nonchalant, "what does it matter, we're all going to die anyway" attitude, which denies any actual reckoning with our earthly path and responsibilities.

Transitory Nature, by contrast, asks us to open up to the full range of body/mind expression, moving beyond egoic attachments and aversions. This requires us to grapple with our extreme psychological and egoic aversion to the expiration date of our own life, and fears about the expiration dates on certain people, places, and situations, which are at the root of so many of our painful experiences. In the above sections, you were guided to touch in with these aversions—beginning to move away from both self-obsessed searches to heal, and existential nonchalance, and into a space where you could acknowledge your Transitory Nature.

Within this exploration, we again see the fundamental binary that births ALL binaries: life/death. When we commit to accepting and honoring Transitory Nature, we begin to break this binary down—understanding the distinctions between unnecessary traumatization and necessary evolution and becoming able to find value in some of these less comfortable states as gateways to transformation and empathy. At the center of our work to break the Sick/Well binary and embrace our Transitory Nature lives one potent question. Hold yourself in softness as you practice asking it:

Why am I so obsessed with "wellness"? When in reality, within my first breath, my grave is marked?

Death is the great equalizer; the ego-structure, the great stratifier. Releasing ourselves from the Sick/Well binary's addictive perfectionism of healing, while reframing our understanding of death, is ultimately what lets us embrace a life of freedom, alignment, and resilience during our limited time on earth. When we practically work to accept death in all areas of our life—physically, emotionally, and psychologically—a different kind of motivation for living arises. One that springs from compassion rather than our ego-structure's avoidance of suffering or illness. We become less obsessed with our personal work and more adept at developing empathy—the ability to see, hear, feel, and appreciate sickness, pain, and trauma—without any violent pushback or reactive judgment in our own system.

The Sick/Well binary runs from and denies death, and we must work to accept it by acknowledging and honoring our own Rites of Passage—all of the deaths we experience throughout our lives. In the ritual sections that follow, we will work practically to accept death in order to uncover our own depths of compassionate action.

The Sick/Well binary espouses a worldview that neglects our emotional maturity in coping with transitions and expiration dates. Bringing awareness to and ritualizing the complexity of your own transitions will diminish your attachment to this binary and help you to embrace your Transitory Nature. While it can be profound to read about ancient Rites of Passage from different cultures, we need rites that are practical, accessible, and workable in our modern lives. With each of the suggested Rites of Passage rituals below there is plenty of room to be creative; each of these rituals will look different based on your personal religious and cultural context.

Rites of Passage for Endings

Mark your transitions first with a goodbye and then a hello. When we move from grade to grade, city to city, job to job, we have a modern cultural habit of throwing a party, eating some cupcakes, and celebrating newness. The closing of the door is not acknowledged, and half of the human range of emotion is bypassed as we are socialized only to "look forward." We can look back to our early socialization around endings and goodbyes and ask ourselves: Were these occasions acknowledged in our childhoods? Did the people around us pass down a clear language, action, and ceremony around letting go and closing a door? Did they take time to reflect and learn from the past?

As a family, parent, or individual in transition, practice implementing a Goodbye Ceremony before any public party or celebration of the new, using this time as one of reflection, respect, love, and admiration for all that has been. Incorporate several steps:

1) *Reminisce about all of the difficulties and successes associated with the entire experience.* Write this down and take note of all these points.

2) *Focus on the emotions that you experienced throughout the entire situation, and the growth points that arose.* Do this in dialogue with self and/or community. Often our memory is selective when recalling past emotional states of attachment. Take your time and be clear with the storyline of emotions that arose from this phase in your life.

3) *Remember that the cyclical process of endings is what frees up new energy for a different beginning.* Write about a time in the past when this was true for you.

4) *Accompany this process with embodied movement and interactive reminiscing.* Get the whole body/mind involved. This is where the creative ceremony may enter. Keep in mind that this doesn't have to be a picture-perfect happy ceremony. In fact, for it to be a potent Rite of Passage, it must exemplify the full range of body/mind emotion.

Your Rites of Passage for Endings will be extremely personal. Try not to reach for commodified ceremony kits or products. Be clear in your own energy: what do you already have within you to answer the above questions and create an interactive reflection and embodied goodbye?

Rites of Passage for Your Changing Body

In many self-help spaces, we attempt to honor the non-linear trajectory of life by using poetic language about life cycles, earth's cycles, and our own internal seasons. Yet, we continue to ignore our body's cycles as we pop painkillers or push through work as our body/mind calls out for attention and recalibration. Breaking the Sick/Well binary and learning to honor the cyclical nature of birth/life/death, requires us to acknowledge our breathing bodies, and to listen to the subtle cycles and shifts that happen within us before they even manifest in the physical realm.

Start here:

1) *Write in detail about how the social context of your upbringing might have hid, buried, or masked your changing body.*

2) *When, if ever, have you identified your unwillingness to accept and acknowledge your changing body/mind?* Think about an instance of illness, injury, or emotional turmoil, or evidence of your body aging, when you became avoidant. Describe in detail how you shoved away a changing reality.

3) *Identify the voice within you that gets frustrated, feels less than, or is addicted to "results," and that desensitizes you to your constantly changing body.* This voice might have several tones, personalities, and inner demands— be clear and deliberate in naming its forms.

4) *Lastly, what sense of self-worth have you built upon shaky ground?* Think of attachment to certain standards of body shape, beauty, youthfulness, and "health" that keep you from accepting a body/mind that is actually built for change.

This Rite of Passage for a Changing Body can become an event of artistic expression and celebration that you might adopt on each birthday, or any time you need clarity around how to stay with your evolving self. Practice deep acceptance and adaptability during these rites, and look out for any tendency that you might have towards avoidance, quick fixes, or self-loathing.

Rites of Passage for Birth/Life/Death Transitions

Every cycle in our lives follows an arcline composed of three distinct phases: Creation/Life Span/Passing. Each one of these phases has its own rhythm, demands a certain energy from us, and asks for a willingness to let go when the time has arrived.

I often remind myself that these can each unfold over extended periods of time, as we process and integrate each phase of the cycle. When we examine relationships, possessions, living spaces, jobs, and projects in our lives from this vantage point, we learn to stop investing our self-worth and personal value in fixed ideas of "success," and start to realize that all of life is one long, extended transition that asks for openness, love, and spiritual maturity. Experiment with honoring this three-part process in all your life situations:

Creative Project Rite of Passage (I use this book project as an example)

1) Inception Moment: the seed for the book was planted
2) Creation Period: three-year period taking steps to put this book out in the world
3) Birth: the day the book actually hits the shelves
4) Mini Death moment: the creation part of the process is over, and a new phase begins
5) Life Phase: the project's countless years out in the world, as others engage with it
6) Mini Death: old me must let go in order to recycle energy to birth a new project
7) Listening for the next Inception Moment ...
8) Preparing for the next high-energy Creation Period ...

Personal Relationship Rite of Passage

1) Inception Moment: you meet another soul whom you will walk next to for a bit
2) Creation Period: excitement, building new intimacy, developing the container of relationship
3) Birth: a new you begins to emerge as this new relationship influences your sense of self

4) Mini Death: old attachments, habits, and psychic hang-ups have to be released for the new you to emerge fully

5) Life Phase: shifting from the newness of Creation phase to a different level of attention that is required to sustain the relationship

6) Mini Death: another shedding process, as you realize you have a limited amount of attention, and that attention must leave other people, places, and things in order to walk with this current relationship for the time being

7) Listening deeply for a reciprocal return on your investment of personal energy. If it's a Full Soul Body "Yes," you are still in the sustenance phase. If it's a Full Soul Body "No," you are headed into the erosion phase.

8) Death: the parting, the letting go, and the extricating yourself from an old solid identity and moving into a form you cannot yet see

You can repeat the above process for any situation you have found yourself in. How do you trace these cycles for yourself? Listen to your ever-changing body/mind with these phases in mind. When I catch myself feeling restless, upset, or rushed, I pull back and get a handle on which phase of the cycle I am currently at odds with and seek to explore why this might be.

Rites of Passage to Accept Your Own Mortality and the Transitory Nature of Others

All of us bounce up against our own aging and the aging of our loved ones at some point. And we all have our own complex story that sits in these spaces, often not confronting our own mortality until we are forced to see it first-hand in our surrounding relationships. If we want to truly break the Sick/Well binary, this is the realization of ALL realizations: LIFE and DEATH are inextricably linked. No matter how "Well" you become, death is the great equalizer. So how do we learn to sit with, honor, and integrate this truth? Start with the exploration of your willingness to accept death, summoning directness, love, and a sense of responsibility as you do so:

1) *What have you confronted, organized, and accepted about your own death?*

Have you arranged for a loving, easy, peaceful way of passing in the physical realm? Do you need help, assistance, or someone else to step in and speak for you legally in case of emergency? Take self-responsibility and agency for your own mortality: can you organize and categorize some physical decisions that would honor your own death? Consider finances, physical belongings, relationships, honoring rituals, and personal needs in this process. Free write creatively around these topics.

2) *Outline your ideal personal death demands.* Please do not feel "selfish" in brainstorming these—those around you who seek to support you in your passing will deeply appreciate your clarity, and it will open space for everyone to grieve.

Revisit these personal inquiries about your willingness to accept the inevitability of death; as your life and values change, so will the answers to these long-term questions. Now let's flip these questions, and look at our loved ones:

1) *Be open and honest with your parents, loved ones, and extended family, whether or not you think they can "handle" it.* Ask if they have a Will in place. Who is the power of attorney on that Will?

2) *Be direct about their financial situation and how they are going to pay for end-of-life care.* Do they need your help? Do they need help arranging finances so they feel empowered in this place?

3) *What do they need and want in their years of passing?* Do they want to be in their home? Do they want to be in hospice? Can you all effectively plan to make this transition a loving one, where the entire family can be present?

We will all have elders to take care of at some point in our lives, biological or not. And many of the logistics get pushed to the end, so that the actual act of letting go becomes filled with organizational tasks that keep us stuck in self-created stress rather than actually dealing with a deeper pain that has evolutionary potential. Be brave with this section. Examine your own mortality first so that you will not confuse a loved one's passing with your own ego-structure-created pain about your own expiration date.

Ultimately, the "wellness" of a society cannot be measured by bio-markers and medical data, but must instead be felt through the empathy and compassionate action that's required to handle transitions with spiritual maturity. Breaking the Sick/Well binary means living a life full of joy, pain, intensity, celebration, transition, and reflection. At times, it might look like the most downright "unhealthy" thing, as you say "cheers" and eat some fried food. At times, it will look like mental illness, as you grapple with the ego-structure's need to feel in control of all transitions. And sometimes, it will look like physical sickness as your body/mind cries out for support, love, assistance, and attention.

Nothing is permanent. How could it be, if we ourselves have an expiration date? These birth/death/life Rites of Passage are intended to connect you with the ever-changing you and your Transitory Nature. When we commit to confronting the ephemeral in our daily actions, we can begin to break the Sick/Well binary: reorienting away from attachment to what fades and towards resiliency.

SUBTLE BODY PRACTICE

Meditative Practice to Accept Your Own Mortality

At its core, silent meditation asks the ego structure to accept its expiration date. When we simply sit in silence, or ZaZen, we are able to observe our ego's fear of zero stimulus.

This is another strategically simple and extremely potent spiritual practice. Because so many of us crave stimulation and thus find silent, seated meditation to be "very challenging," it is worth doing with care and attention. Here is how I often describe it to many of my students:

Sit down
Shut up
Observe
Nothing fancy here
Repeat

Posture

Sit in sukhasana, or a simple, cross-legged seat. Prop yourself, if necessary, to support your body. If you experience knee pain, you can always straighten your legs and support your lower back or sit in a chair. We will revisit this architecture of peace several times in this text.

Mudra

Mudra literally translates as "seal": a position of the body that creates a sealed circuit of flowing energy. In the context of this text, it is used in relation to hand mudras. For this chapter's practice, the palms are face down, and the arms and elbows are relaxed, hanging near the side of the body.

Timing

Practice 10 minutes daily for 30+ consecutive days.

Immediately after your 10-minute Zazen sit, pick up your pen and notepad and explore these questions in all realms—physical, emotional, psychological, and spiritual—with precision, and without self-editing your answers:

What did I Birth today?
What did I Sustain today?
What did I Kill today?

THE THIRD BINARY
MASCULINE/FEMININE: BODY AS VEHICLE

They often approach me in session with this deep yearning to be someone else: something more acceptable by another's standards. Which often means someone more feminine, or something more masculine.

In session, they say to me: "He left me because I was too intense; I think I need to be more feminine, can you help me do that?" In another session, they say to me: "Most people accuse me of being hyper-sensitive; am I too much in my feminine? How do I bring more masculinity into my life?"

It's poking out—this gross flubbery thing that's always giving me anxiety. Adjust belt, suck it in, make it rock hard, turn sideways, did they see?

Hiding in plain sight. Slumping, caving in at the heart to protect my vulnerability. Wishing I was different. Wishing for acceptance.

Eyes on me, I can feel it. They covet my body. I can use it to get what I want. Flaunt my sexy eyes. Flex, show off my muscles.

Take a moment, close your eyes, and connect to your own lived experience. What emotions are stirring in your body as you remember how it feels to be assessed by the sum of your physical parts? What would it be like to move through the world without the societal pressure to look and behave a certain way based on your gender expression?

On some level we all have felt deep displacement within our own physical form. These are the unspoken moments when we sense society's implicit gender bias; and on a painful, unconscious level we each absorb this into our own identities, allowing that judgment to infiltrate our sacred relationship to self. *Displaced in our own homes: our bodies.* Before we have even taken our first inhalation, the world, our parents, our family units, and our communities have already projected a heavy burden onto our identity. It is the very first binary that forcibly penetrates our self-identity: Masculine/Feminine.

Awwww, you're having a girl? She'll grow up to be so pretty just like you!
Ohhhhh, you're having a girl—they're so emotional and hard to deal with

Awwww, you're having a boy? Gotta teach him how to throw a spiral!
Ohhhhh, you're having a boy—he's gonna be a ladies man just like his dad

This hypothetical picture of who we are and how we should behave, based on a gendered perception of our biological sex—as well as the psychosocial implications of that initial perception—predates our own embodied experience of self. And it influences our perspective on EVERYTHING. Each and every aspect of our lived experience is filtered through the lens of the Masculine/Feminine binary.

We are force-fed narratives of "who we think we are" before we have the full capacity to reason and discern from our actual embodied experience. Instead of being able to use our bodies as vehicles for creative, unbridled expression, fueled by the wisdom of self-knowledge, we arrive into a predestined experience of our bodies—with labels, do's and don'ts, and acceptable and rejectable identities.

The Masculine/Feminine binary is like a social software update that we do not consent to, and we bump up against the perceived power dynamics of this binary in our family units, partnerships, parenting, and professions. This binary is embedded within the intimacy of the self-identity landscape, and the hidden beliefs by which we organize our existence and present ourselves to the world. This element of binary worldview has been shaped by years of oppressive heteropatriarchy in cultures all over the globe, fed by the incessant need to maintain gendered hierarchies and protect population growth within power hungry social systems that limit our consciousness expansion and stifle deep creative expression.

The Masculine/Feminine binary is inextricably situated in larger, vital conversations about gender identity, gender expression, biology, sexuality, and social inequality. In reality, even biological sex cannot be conceived or defined apart from cultural understandings. The work of non-binary worldview sees gender as fluid, and honors the incredible strides made by those—especially in the transgender community—to shift how we see these concepts and our cultural attachment to cissexism.

In new age spirituality and wellness circles, the binary is often hidden in flowery language and propped up by the mention of ancient teachings, archetypes, and religious myths. For example, our current conversations about self-care, self-love, and self-acceptance often lean heavily on a reductive, materialistic, and Feminine binary approach. Let's begin our work of dismantling the third binary by defining our misaligned understandings of the Masculine and Feminine principles:

Binary Masculine relies on aggressive, extractive, and power-hungry behavior, the devaluing of emotions, the need to be right, addiction to the physical and the intellectual, rigidity, and the repression of creativity and our expressive natures. In this chapter, I will use terms like Hyper-Masculinity and Toxic Masculinity to sum up these attributes.

Binary Feminine relies on service at the detriment of self, people pleasing, body-centric suffering and manipulation, being the receiver to a fault, heightened emotional sensitivity that's seen as weak, and victimhood mentality. I will use terms like Hyper-Femininity and Manipulative Femininity to sum up these attributes.

These are the subconscious gender projections and energetic internalizations that arise out of a cis-normative heteropatriarchy. We have all internalized these binary understandings of the Masculine and Feminine prin-

75

ciples, leading to so much self-hatred as the result of perceived judgments about our physicality. Spiritual Agency around our unique identity is lost, creativity is destroyed, and curiosity about who we really are is banished.

Our willingness to break the Masculine/Feminine binary asks us to question how culture shapes our understanding of our bodies, our value, our appearance, our merger with other souls, and our purposefully unique work in the world. This chapter will ask you to examine all of the places the Masculine/Feminine binary hides within you—the places where, as a result, you are separated from your creative life-giving essence in its truest form.

You may sense many "snap" reactions to my words in this chapter, because examining these deeply held beliefs often challenges the existing framework of how you value yourself and derive meaning from life events. I am asking you to mindfully examine that millisecond gap before the "snap" so you can move yourself beyond the Masculine/Feminine binary—in turn allowing yourself, and every other human, to live from a place of pure freedom that makes space for many identities, and restores the beauty and complexity of the human experience. After this interrogation and dismantling of the binary, we will start to build a constructive model for viewing self and other that tactfully uses the technology of the body and its spiritual skills as a deeply aware, transformative "vehicle" for a genderless expression of power and pure creativity.

At the beginning of the second millennium we are traveling through the Kali Yuga—a time of deep spiritual darkness, death, and transformation that requires us to acknowledge and consciously participate in a cyclical dissolution and reconstruction of ourselves, our values, and our socio-political organizations. During this intensely evolutionary time, it is only when we commit to breaking the Masculine/Feminine binary that we will learn to relate to our bodies as vehicles for creating true societal change.

THE MYTHS OF MASCULINE/FEMININE

The Dual Identity Myth
We all have Masculine and Feminine within us

Countless coaches, self-help experts, and healers use this statement, thereby setting up a "marriage of opposites" approach. This seems liberatory on the surface, but it actually reinforces limiting cissexism and heteropatriarchal either/or-ness, reducing our capacity to reimagine a world where oppression based on gender identity or expression does not exist. Within non-binary worldview we must be willing to contemplate our attachment to the very terms "Masculine" and "Feminine," not because they are rooted in transcendent reality, but because we have been socialized to believe them as reality.

I have seen this dual identity myth cause deep pain within my students, as they struggle by bouncing between extremes—over-compensating and pushing themselves into an "accepted" identity within the Masculine/Feminine binary. As students explore the Feminine, they ask pandering questions that cling to reductionist understandings of this principle: "Should I wear more skirts?"; "What Goddesses should I work with?"; "How can I be more sensual in my daily life?" I even hear many a being who identifies as "she," blindly submitting to heteropatriarchal abuse in the name of their own healing.

And at the other end of the binary, I see struggles to downplay or repress certain "Masculine" behaviors for fear that they'll be demonized, alienated, or written off as unforgiving and cold. In fact, many of our modern self-help healing spaces are constructed entirely on the idea of "resurrecting the Feminine," which only reinforces binary worldview and severs each of us from the full totality of expression. This dualistic understanding, and the definitions of Masculine and Feminine within it, often draw from misinterpretations of ancient teachings. Terms like Shiva/Shakti and Yin/Yang are quickly adopted into our Masculine/Feminine binary vernacular, bolstering reductive binary worldview with spiritual claims.

Within their original context, Shiva/Shakti are discussed as impersonal, universal energies that are two aspects of the same "it" that is genderless—a neuter noun that describes inseparable attributes of the same principle and is not associated with or depicted through the human body. We often see these terms used out of context, morphed to fit a binary heteropatriarchal understanding of Masculine and Feminine, with "Shiva" taking on the binary Masculine qualities of structure and holding, and "Shakti" often referred to as the binary Feminine personified.

Similarly, Yin/Yang—a principle that expresses the higher power in Taoism—attempts to communicate that all forms contain the other side of their polarity. "Yin" and "Yang" are not totally opposite from one another, but create a spectrum of relativity given the context. Taken together, they demonstrate that the higher power is beyond limiting views of duality. And yet, again, we have a tendency to anthropomorphize these concepts and to reduce Yin to represent the Feminine and Yang, the Masculine. These terms aren't inherently gendered; it is the organizing principles of our consciousness that genders them.

Our very own societal self-concept perpetuates this myth. When we buy into this vision of "dualism," fetishizing limited "desirable" versions of both Masculine and Feminine, we are setting the self-improvement stage with immature archetypes that continue to limit our consciousness growth and sever our connection to the genderless creative essence that rests within all of us. And underneath the binaried understanding of the "Divine Feminine" and "Sacred Masculine" principles (which in Hindu scriptures are often depicted as embodying all gender attributes) lie hyper-gendered archetypes that actually perpetuate the heteronormative patriarchy.

By contract, within non-binary worldview we aren't seeking to simply marry the opposites; we are seeking to create an identity that transcends duality entirely. This means defining ourselves differently, so that we can assert our creative energy differently—asking the world to know us by our creative essence rather than societal projections of gender.

The Wild Woman Myth

Picture this: *A ciswoman wearing slightly revealing clothing. Breast and hip centered movements coming from her body. Perhaps some red lipstick, wild hair, lots of jewelry, makeup, and a high-end manicure. She is using her voice with power, employing words like "reclaiming," "cycles," "non-linear healing," and voicing how we might rise up against the patriarchy.*

We commonly encounter this binaried interpretation of the "Divine Feminine" archetype, which preaches to be revolutionary and inclusive. Yet often these representations reproduce heteronormative and heteropatri- archal ideals, while making audacious claims that Wild Woman work is for everyone regardless of how they identify. Beneath a vision of "reawak- ening the Wild Woman archetype" lie cis-normative, ableist, sexist, racist beauty standards that ultimately only perpetuate oppression. Our pleas- ure, our perceived freedom, and our boundless creativity remain limited by how deeply the heteropatriarchy has infiltrated women's gaze upon themselves and others.

While the second-wave feminist movement of the 1970s encouraged women to burn their bras, eschew makeup, and let their body hair grow out in the name of invoking the "goddess," heteronormative sexist beau- ty standards have crept back into our current commercialized facade of female empowerment. After all, selfies with cleavage get the most likes and reshares on social media, many under the guise of "empowerment." Hyper-sexualizing the female form is exactly what the heteropatriarchy wants! Filtered through this lens, its focus on "reclaiming" female sexual- ity means the modern Wild Woman Myth has come to reinforce a limited view of sex and its potential to create powerful intimacy and expressive freedom among all bodies.

Even more dangerously, by equating "freedom" and "personal em- powerment" with provocative displays of wanton flesh by certain bodies deemed "acceptable," we are continuing to oppress both ciswomen and a vision of the Feminine and its power that can be expressed by *any* body.

I can already sense the push back:

It's my right to be in my pleasure
I want to share my body with the world in the way that I want
You can't tell me how to use my body—it's mine!

Working through misperceptions of hyper-sexuality, the female body as capital, past sexual trauma, and how and why you experience pleasure in your physical form, are all necessary steps in evolving the Feminine end of the binary. As we work through these misperceptions, we need to pay close attention to where acts of reclamation may actually perpetuate racist, sexist, ableist, cis-normative standards of domination.

The Wild Woman Myth is also linked to the problematic Maiden/Mother binary. Within this binary, we see the "Maiden" portrayed as an innocently sexy, playful figure frolicking in the fields—implying that youth, fertility, and provocation are qualities to be celebrated, and are necessary to develop if we want to be accepted. And within the aging "Mother" archetype, we are told that true maturity and service come from putting aside the expressive creativity of the Maiden as we step into motherhood, and women's "natural" role as nurturers.

At both ends of this binary, creative force is seen as synonymous with child-bearing fertility and feminine maturity with child-rearing responsibilities. Within binary worldview, we're told that if we have the biology to do so, motherhood is the ultimate in fulfilment. And once we achieve this by leaving the Maiden archetype behind to bear children, paradoxically, our bodies become less acceptable at best, and entirely expendable at worst.

And if we choose not to have children, questions are sure to arise as others wonder if our body is healthy, assuring us that "It will happen one day, don't worry," and making moral judgments based on their own choices because: *How could a woman not want to be a mother?* In all of these conversations, the regenerative creativity embodied in the Wild Woman Myth continues to be equated with pro-generation itself—alienating all of us from the freedom for all beings, regardless of gender expression or biology, to express "birthing" energy of all kinds.

The Sensitive Man Myth

In many ways, the commercialized Wild Woman has been constructed as a "savior" for the suffering perpetrated by the patriarchy—while often perpetuating this same suffering in a different costume. At the other end of the binary, the Masculine's answer to this suffering becomes the Sensitive Man, which comes with its own limitations that keep us trapped in binary worldview.

The Sensitive Man tends to look like a human who embodies "manly" qualities of rugged physicality and identifies as "he," but who also displays a soft sensitivity. This "soft edge" is seen as part of the "Feminine" within binary worldview. By ascribing to the notion that Toxic Masculinity can be "saved" by sprinkling in a little emotion and sensitivity, we avoid any deep reckoning with the binary itself, suggesting that "men just need to get in touch with their Feminine side."

By suggesting that the Sensitive Man is more elevated because of a connection to emotional sensitivity that's part of the so-called binary Feminine, we also put the Feminine on a pedestal, claiming that it is more "enlightened" while hiding the aspects of it that remain unexamined. I've seen countless male-identified students who struggle to "evolve" by connecting to their emotions, chasing the end goal of an idealized Feminine principle while also attempting to uphold the so-called Masculine principles of grounded space holding, without having any real embodied knowledge of how to express emotions.

"Sacred Masculine" energy is supposedly rooted in the concepts of stability, grounded energy, and the capacity to "be a container." Yet within this definition of the Sensitive Man, we still see certain assumptions about handsomeness, and about occupational and body standards that are connected to a vision of a well-groomed, tall, muscular, cisman who fulfills the role of "provider" as defined by capitalist standards.

Through the filter of the Masculine/Feminine binary, the rhetoric goes: "Look like a strong cisman, but sport a man bun to embody your Feminine. Be approachable, but not a pushover!" We see countless representations of what the so-called "enlightened" Sensitive Man is supposed to look like in popular culture, whether it's the sexy mountain man who's connected to nature, or the powerful CEO with a heart of gold. But OMG these more superficial attempts to adopt supposedly Feminine principles actually perpetuate a reductive understanding of both Masculine and Feminine. Within this context, a battle is being waged between Toxic Masculinity and its apparent opposite, Sensitive Masculinity. This actually obscures the fact that simply attempting to integrate Masculine and Feminine is not the answer to transcending the binary, which is what we must do if all beings are to have access to learning and expressing these profoundly compassionate aspects of human energetics.

We also see this in the emergence of the "Guru Archetype" or "Wise Teacher." Historically, these positions are held by someone who identifies as "he," but who plays down Hyper-Masculine behavior by using words that appear to be "sacred" and publicly showing emotional sensitivity—a mythos that has proven to be rife with abuse, inflicted by these same teachers upon vulnerable students of all gender expressions.

As we attempt to course correct, we are seeing the rise of those who identify as "she" holding the seat of teacher, which is wonderful in terms of more access, representation, and shifting the mainstream narrative. Yet just as the Wild Woman is sometimes an unconscious byproduct of the Hyper-Masculine patriarchy, the Sensitive Man "push back" against Toxic Masculinity often shames many cismen and masculine-identifying people away from supposedly open and inclusive spaces of self-study and personal growth.

As you can see, at both ends of the Masculine/Feminine binary, we are faced with immature, highly categorical, inherently violent notions of Masculine, Feminine, and even dual identity. Misappropriated ancient spiritual teachings are used in service of oppressive, patriarchal, cis-normative systems—perpetuating violence, cutting us off from a true understanding of human consciousness, and creating deep divisions within supposed "healing communities." Now that we've begun to grapple with some of the most damaging mainstream myths about the Masculine and Feminine, let's turn inward to explore how these principles manifest in our daily lives. Then we'll shift our gaze from a deconstructive model of inquiry to a constructive one, building a regenerative self-identity based in genderless creativity.

PERSONAL INQUIRY PRACTICE:
THE TOXIC MASCULINE + MANIPULATIVE FEMININE

Please don't limit me
With your conditioned view of yourself

He, She, they, them, brilliantly an individual
A phoenix

Rising from the ashes
Free of category
Liberated from hierarchy
Fluid in self understanding
Powerful in self-expression

Care to join me?
The whole world waits
And when you do,
A deep communal sigh
For we all feel
Freedom in our bodies

In keeping with the Wild Woman Myth (explored above), we often see lists of "positive" attributes associated with the Feminine principle that we are tasked with "reclaiming"—such as emotion, intuition, embodiment, pleasure, and receptivity. In contrast, we often see Toxic Masculinity spelled out in a list of "negative" attributes that we must "dismantle," like rigidity, domination, lack of empathy, narrow focus, and aggression. In this section, you will start to look at your own "automatic software downloads" surrounding the Masculine/Feminine binary, bearing witness to how you project these social constructs onto self and others. This "programming" can occur in all parts of our lives—from intimate relationships where the Masculine/Feminine binary limits our personal growth and ability to bear witness to others' fluidity, to professional expectations about which attributes must be suppressed and which are needed to succeed and "get ahead."

Chances are that you will not be able to answer the following questions in one sitting or by using your intellect alone. Often our misperception of the Masculine/Feminine binary runs so deep that trauma, body hate, lack of trust, intimacy issues, anger, and repetitive destructive behavior arise in response to attempts to dismantle it. As such, be gentle with yourself as you dive deep into your gendered psyche using the inquiry presented in this section. To begin, let's clearly define the Manipulative Feminine and its deepest subconscious imprints on the subtle body:

- Victimhood mentality is the resting state
- Energetically needy
- Difficulty setting boundaries
- Internal dissonance that rationalizes realities with emotions, claiming "I feel X, so it MUST be true"
- Manipulative use of the body and sexuality
- Over-giving to boost self-worth and feel needed
- Self-punishing
- Martyr complex

Where and when do you witness, mimic, adopt, and replay these Manipulative Feminine tendencies? Look at the list above and revisit your childhood, adolescence, and early adult life, asking: how did I learn these behaviors?

In what ways do I adopt any of these behaviors to protect my own heart/innocence?

Which influential archetypes in my life modelled these behaviors? In my family, my school, my communities?

In my adult life, where can I take responsibility for some of these Manipulative Feminine tendencies?

Now, let's define the Toxic Masculine and its deepest subconscious imprints on the subtle body:

- Addiction to power; use of the body to assert power dynamics
- Controlling behavior in all contexts

- Attachment to status
- Saving face to portray success
- Over-effort leading to burnout
- Rigidity in thought, form, and body
- Absence of emotion
- Directs self-hatred outward: hyper-critical of others to build up ego-structure

Where and when do you witness, mimic, adopt, and replay these Toxic Masculine tendencies? Look at the list above, and revisit your childhood, adolescence, and early adult life, asking again: how did I learn these behaviors?

In what ways do I adopt any of these behaviors to protect my own heart/innocence?

Which influential archetypes in my life modelled these behaviors? In my family, my school, my communities?

In my adult life, where can I take responsibility for some of these Toxic Masculine tendencies?

Take both lists of attributes and questions into your life flow for a month. Seek out the expression of these attributes within yourself, as well as within your personal and professional contexts. These demons might have different heads, but chances are they will express from the same energetic root. Answer these questions multiple times in reference to Manipulative Feminine and Toxic Masculine attributes. The objective is to get clarity around how you unconsciously contribute to the underbelly of the Masculine/Feminine binary.

These reflections will also help us get a close look at our own "Mother" and/or "Father" wounds—bringing awareness to outdated, abusive programming that has shaped how we express our spirit's deepest yearnings. Committing to this work lets us try on new behaviors and actions with less attachment to past conditions, thereby integrating past pain and perpetuating less of it in the future—for ourselves and for all those in our family line.

I am sensing that a lot of tears, anger, poetry, and peace will arise from these inquiries.

Be brave and go gently as you experiment with your own genderless expressive integrity.

BREAKING THE BINARY: BODY AS VEHICLE

The human form is the most technologically advanced mechanism on earth: systems upon systems that integrate with seamless intelligence. Its adaptability is astounding. And every time we "label it" through categorization, we diminish its innate wisdom. Breaking the Masculine/Feminine binary means restoring this badass piece of technology to its rightful use as a vehicle for expressing our limitless, genderless, divine, creative potential—an open chariot from which to witness social constructs and move beyond them to connect with the highest of truths.

Body As Vehicle creates a fluid new relationship to self-identity by dislodging cultural imprints that have unconsciously infiltrated our flesh suits. We can clearly see how, when, and where we have allowed our body to absorb unchecked software downloads from society. Better yet, we can see where we have become deeply attached to false narratives, and unconsciously weaponized these modes of behavior against others. With this clarity, we begin to be able to share our bodies as ever-changing, uncategorized, expressions of divinity. This Body As Vehicle awareness is free of shame, free of pretense, and recognizes immense respect for its own power.

Developing Body As Vehicle awareness means contacting the deepest points of misperception within us—doing the revolutionary work of uncovering subliminal messages from culture, family units, and educational and medical systems. Seeing our Body as Vehicle challenges our subconscious software updates around gender identity and expression, and changes our embodied electromagnetic frequency around Masculine and Feminine symbols so that we can "plug in" in a new way. Let's get started ...

The following practice, which I've taught on many closed retreats, is rooted in a meditation I learned while I was a student within a celibate spiritual community. Through this two-year practice of celibacy, I was able to cultivate a more genderless creative expression that I had stored over time—not released, given away, or misused. While I know celibacy is not the path for everyone, you can connect to this energy by committing to engage in this practice alone; you will need privacy to really explore and not feel limited by the social structures of company or community.

As you begin this 30-day practice, revisit the archetypes that come up for you as you review the list of Manipulative Feminine and Toxic Masculine traits, and engage the contemplative questions in the Personal Inquiry section above. This practice is intended to help you consciously move through subconscious holdings that keep us attached to the underbelly of the Masculine/Feminine binary, allowing you to literally "see" exactly where these archetypes live and how they express in *your* body. We must move "through them" to transcend them.

Archetype Mirror Work

Find yourself a safe, comfortable space where you can have some privacy, in front of a full-length mirror.

1) *Create your embodied archetype.* Building on your work in the Personal Inquiry section, create a character, vision, posture, voice tone, gaze, and set of movements that embody how you experience some of the traits on the Manipulative Feminine and Toxic Masculine lists. Go to the extreme and make it personal. For example, maybe you're ready to work through your Manipulative Feminine's need to be needed by speaking aloud the endless texts you've sent in an emotionally accusatory tone. Or by taking your body through the passes of running up the stairs to bang on your lover's door because you needed closure.

2) *Dance, jump, yell.* Use your body to express and act this out in front of the mirror. Give this several tries. If you feel uncomfortable because the practice feels "weird" ... do it anyway! Any discomfort belies the subconscious attachment to the pain and conditioning

underneath these behaviors, and now is the time to let it out to play. Let this discomfort be evidence of how "unnatural" this gendered stereotype actually is for your body to express.

3) *Integrate.* Feel the cumbersome nature of this costume—the pain this archetype carries as it tries to hold up its facade. Feel the weight this character/person carries in their bones, knowing that it has hurt you and others. Feel, sympathize, forgive the transgressions. You can do this with movement, writing, song, tears, and poetry.

4) *Shapeshift.* Transforming the body into a vehicle means giving it permission to play. Feel free to change forms and postures, moving from energy to energy without holding anything long enough to create emotional residue or mental affliction. Do all of this in front of the mirror, watching yourself in all of your majesty. Notice how it feels to experience the fleeting nature of existence beyond the Masculine/Feminine binary.

Thirty, forty-five, sixty minutes in, when you feel exhausted, REST. Be silent. Lie on the floor and put your legs up the wall. Get comfortable. Place both hands on your power center, just below the navel and above the pubis, in the lake of the belly. Bear witness for five to fifteen minutes after your mirror work. There is no analytical instruction here. Simply let your body settle and hear yourself, and notice the unbridled expressions that break through subconscious holding. Deliberately close your energetic field and increase your sense of safety by putting all professional demands and requests from others aside during this time.

Repeat this exercise two to three times per week over the course of this month's inquiry. Learning, exploring, and embodying new ways of being is a cumulative process that will begin to shift how you see your identity and how you behave in the world. Let your mirror work evolve as you begin to use your body as a divine technology to express beyond the social prison of the Masculine/Feminine binary and come closer to connecting with your genderless spirit.

Reinvent Your Language

As you engage in this deep archetypal mirror work, you can simultaneously work to strip the body of its psychosocial gendering and to re-envision it as a vehicle for universal attributes of human consciousness by noticing and evolving your language. For example: creativity, intuition, body-love, cyclical understanding, and deep connection ARE NOT INHERENTLY FEMININE. Focus, drive, passion, determination, holding a container, and stable energy ARE NOT INHERENTLY MASCULINE.

These are all aspects of the human/spirit identity that exist beyond the social construct of gender—that belong to the higher octaves of all human consciousness. If we continue to gender them, we limit access to evolutionary spaces, preventing all bodies from expressing their full, powerful capacity. How we speak shapes our realities. Make a commitment to yourself to stop gendering universal attributes in your language when speaking of others and when referring to yourself. Use names in place of pronouns, celebrate uniqueness, and describe yourself and others by the universal, non-binary attributes that actually expand consciousness. This alone will shift your neuro linguistic understanding of self and your reality construction.

Develop Universal Attributes of Human Consciousness

As you reinvent your language and start celebrating the limitless potential of yourself and others, you can use the below list of "Universal Attributes of Human Consciousness" to further shift beyond the Masculine/Feminine binary. If we keep doing the inner work to excavate where Manipulative Femininity and Toxic Masculinity live within our own lives, as outlined in the Personal Inquiry section, these universal human attributes of higher consciousness will rise to the surface. Do not rush this process. And stay focused on the outer world shifts you see as the result of doing this intimate inner work.

Creativity

You know it's moving with freedom when it does not seek external validation.

Discernment
You sense its presence when emotion is informative and action reflects non-attachment to outcomes.

Intimacy
A truthful soul connection that is no longer solely attached to body and physical form.

Passion/Compassion
A level of care for another's well-being without any conditions or strings attached.

Empathy
Making space for another's lived experience without comparing it to your own in order to "value or devalue" it.

Determination
Committing to the deep feeling and intensity of sharing your true gender-less spirit with the Universe.

Sensitivity
The capacity to sense the unspoken communication of all interpersonal narratives and consciousness structures.

Intuition
Pure receptivity through deep existential listening.

Equanimity
Meeting each moment as neither Masculine nor Feminine, but with resilience and cohesiveness.

Openness
Last but not least, the checks and balances system for the ego-structure. Remind yourself frequently that you might be WRONG—and that this is

not a reflection of your self-worth but instead an assertion of your willingness to be humble and honor the multiple truths presenting.

Welcome to your radiant, loving, fluid home: Body as Vehicle. May we all seek to set ourselves and others free from the social prison of gender, as we break the Masculine/Feminine binary through lived action and novel structures of consciousness.

SUBTLE BODY PRACTICE

Recalibration Breathwork + Meditation

Processing and freeing ourselves from the shackles of the Masculine/Feminine binary's subliminal software downloads takes a tremendous amount of life force energy! After our Archetype Mirror work, we need to "come down"—allowing the intensity to settle. This intense physical practice is paired with a central nervous system recalibration technique. This is a meditation and pranayam of little physical effort but great mental focus—meaning there is absolutely no reason to over-exert yourself when practicing this breath pattern. Drop all striving from your body/mind as you follow your breath. Pranayam literally translates to the regulation of energy or life force; in this case the breath is reflective of the movement of life force. In the subtle realm, pranayama practices are said to purify the energy channels.

Posture

Sit in sukhasana, or a simple, cross-legged seat. Prop yourself, if necessary, to support your body. Make this easy on your posture and feel free to lean against something. If knee pain is present, you can always straighten your legs and support your lower back or sit in a chair.

Breath Rhythm

Inhalation is separated into 10 consecutive sips. Sense the filling up of the lungs by dividing the long inhalation into 10 deliberate sections that culminate at the very top of the breath. Fill your lungs and relax your face and spine at the top of this 10-part inhalation. After the last sip of the 10-

part inhalation, the palms come together at the forehead; follow a long, slow stable exhalation as you trace the centerline of the body with Añjali (prayer pose) mudra (see opposite).

Inhalation Mudra

Palms face up, open and relaxed, with fingers together during the inhalation pattern. With each breath sip, incrementally move the open palms upward, timed with each breath segment. Elbows are bent and remain relaxed with each upward action of the palms.

At the top of the breath on the final inhalation segment, bring hands to touch in prayer pose in front of forehead.

Exhalation Mudra

As the exhalation begins, slowly and ceremonially descend the prayer pose mudra along the central channel of the body, matching one long fluid exhalation. Anjali mudra (prayer pose): may my heart be soft, open, and compassionate.

Pause at the bottom in Gyan mudra (your Jupiter, or index finger, is touching the thumb, as pictured in the third image opposite) as the breath cycle completes and you rest at the bottom of the breath.

Then repeat the 10-sip inhalation, with accompanying open palm mudra. Prayer pose mudra at the top of the breath in front of the forehead, descend prayer pose mudra down the centerline of the body with exhalation pattern. Pause in gyan mudra at the bottom of the breath.

Timing

Practice 3 focused minutes daily for 30+ consecutive days.

II.
LIVING
HEART
ACTION

THE FOURTH BINARY
LACK/ABUNDANCE: PRANIC ECONOMY

Lindsay, a long-time student of mine, was raised in a "hardworking," emotionally disconnected family. Extremely sensitive and intuitive, with a love of service, she'd established a dedicated track record within her corporate spheres, doing excellent work and often picking up co-workers' slack.

Working long hours for years in the corporate world was all she knew—it felt safe. She had created a relatively peaceful life for herself. But while she looked "okay" to the rest of the world, she felt a deep severing within, often expressing to me that she felt disempowered and voiceless in certain parts of her life. These feelings would arise with an unsettled stirring of discontentment, as if she were denying her true nature by fitting herself into the corporate mold day-in and day-out. A voice within her psyche would occasionally knock, whispering the truth in an unmistakable tone. It was that voice that she longed to listen to and act upon.

Lindsay was reaching a common crossroads on the path of living her spirituality—a crossroads where many beings wake up and begin to seek alignment within the many facets of their personal and professional lives. Rationalizations of her work that were previously allowed in her physical/spiritual system were now registering as out of alignment with her personal growth. Lindsay was slowly beginning to realize that some of her previous life choices were deeply disrespectful to her own creative resources, as well as to the loved ones and relationships that surrounded her.

Yet each time she decided, *Okay, now is the time I'm going to make a change*, and began to gather the courage to walk away from the morally compromising environment of corporate America, the boundaries of the Lack/

Abundance binary would create a hard and fast stop in her trajectory of awakening. Misperceptions about how she made her money, and an addiction to conformity and safety, would take center stage, and the self-worth and personal power necessary to build a new life would be snuffed out every time. Lindsey believed that Abundance was only available within a binary worldview based on Lack.

Each time she attempted to expand, Lindsay's "Lack glass ceiling" reared its head through thoughts and actions, which included:

- Valuing herself through a hyper-material lens and underestimating the intrinsic value of her personal creative resources.
- Constantly replaying self-diminishing thoughts and moments of failure and feeling "less than," thereby reinforcing an embodied state of Lack.
- Dismissing her Lack narrative with personal excuses and abuses, like convincing herself that self-punishment was the answer, when in actuality it was moving her further out of balance and deeper into Lack.
- Resting in her own attachment to the Lack narrative because it felt safe; taking no actions and allowing this self-defeating mentality to win.

In every impulse purchase, in your exhaustion at the end of the day, in the feeling of being "trapped" in a relationship or job role, the Lack/Abundance binary is present. Within this binary worldview, we attempt to create Abundance by moving away from feelings of Lack. Yet by simply running from our fears of Lack, we do very little to deal with what is actually lacking within us. Many of us end up believing that simply getting "more" will fill the gaps. In our constant attempt to acquire more, we bring our Lack with us, chasing unsustainable, lack-based notions of Abundance that discount the health of the entire economic ecosystem.

The feeling of "less than" motivates our personal spending habits, family values, sales and marketing techniques, business models and, at our core, our very own understanding of ourselves. We see Abundance as a metric that measures how much "stuff" we can acquire, how much power we can gain, and how big our companies and bank accounts can become. And in the process, we create a stratified economic system that deepens the fear-based divides between the "haves" and the "have-nots."

This limited binary thinking relates human purpose to productivity and cash flow, thus oppressing two of our most valuable resources: imagination and creativity.

Do any of these common thought/action patterns sound familiar?

I have to charge less because I feel like I am not worth more

I am barely making ends meet, but I am too scared of rejection to ask for more money

I need to get the name and branding perfect before I can charge more

I love doing this but I'm anxious all the time because I am not getting the numbers I need

I can hear the anxious, Lack-based Abundance meta-dialogue firing within you already:

I may have enough today, but what about my future?

If I opt out of this paradigm, my resources will drain away and I'll be left destitute

In the face of a modern global economy that insists on productivity at all costs, how do we break the Lack/Abundance binary? The answer lies in cultivating an understanding of sustainable Abundance that is grounded in the human and earthly resources that exist beyond the material, and in learning to honor our bodies, our sacred time, and the Earth itself.

The conversations in this chapter won't be around "making it big," or "attracting more Abundance into our lives." *The answer isn't simply to move from "Lack" to "Abundance."* Or to solely bring more Abundance into your own life while neglecting the impact of this on the larger economic ecosystem. Instead, we will use our imaginations to dismantle the Lack/Abundance binary, creating anew by learning to live in the shades of gray.

We'll begin by identifying all the ways we perpetuate the Lack/Abundance binary in our own lives. Through an exploration of our meta-dialogue, we'll start to recognize what thoughts and actions keep us swinging between states of depletion and numbed-out consumerism. And from this space of reckoning, we will courageously commit to laying the groundwork for a "Pranic Economy" that cultivates self-worth and an embodied reevaluation of our human and earthly resources, encouraging a true sharing economy where everybody gets to thrive.

THE MYTHS OF LACK/ABUNDANCE

The More Is Better Myth

You ask spirit: *Can I have some more please?*
But what exactly are you asking for "more" of? Money? Stuff? Love? Ease? Clients? Happiness?

At this time in our evolution, human beings are more materially comfortable overall than we have ever been. Yet despite living in the lap of convenience, many of us still feel "less than." And by only addressing the Abundance end of the binary (our unconscious drive to keep amassing "more" even when we have "enough"), these ideas reinforce what is already an imbalance within our psyches, which then perpetuates massive societal inequality.

Within the current cultural Lack/Abundance binary, we are constantly being overfed and undernourished. Always plugged in and consuming "empty calories" beyond what our sense portals actually need. This cycle of consumerism itself dulls human creativity, atrophying resourcefulness, our self-reliance, and the ability to discern what we really need.

Consider a simple spending cycle:

Bored and discontent, you find yourself aimlessly scrolling online stores. As you do so, you are prodded by images and copy that tacitly define you as "less than." You "need" this item if you want to look like her. It is this month's "must have" that will gain you acceptance. Before you know it, you have been leached of your personal resources, while nothing has been done to address the underlying "boredom and discontent" that led to the purchase.

Will this consumerist loop be unwound anytime soon, given our global climate? Absolutely not. But in cultivating awareness around how we engage with it, we can start to dismantle it from the inside out. What if "more" doesn't mean money, stuff, or even confidence? What if "more" means the personal objectivity to see through our own Lack mentality? May I have more clarity about what I actually "need," please?

Ask Yourself:
What is the dominant feeling attached to an urge to spend or acquire?
What inner truth am I actually avoiding by "spending" energy in this way?
What are the qualities of the source from which I am about to consume?
Is this a sustainable energetic exchange? Am I getting my "energy's worth"?

What's a "sustainable" exchange? Every single time you receive or spend human and earthly resources, it is part of a life/death/rebirth cycle. Assessing and honoring where your energy is in this cycle, and the interconnectivity between its parts, helps keep things sustainable. If I've just birthed a project, I recognize that old Lack-based wounds had to die to bring it to life. And if I feel a hungry impulse to immediately birth another effort right away, I remind myself that my resources are needed to sustain the life of the current project. When we underestimate the worthiness of the phase we're in we underestimate our own worth, spreading ourselves thin and shifting from sustainable Abundance to Lack-based Abundance.

Each time you expend resources, ask yourself the following. *On a physical, emotional, and psychic level: What dies? What is birthed? What is sustained?*

These lines of inquiry help reveal where we might be wasting resources and overstaying an obvious expiration date within a relationship or job, addicted to a Lack narrative that's grounded in personal egoic attachment rather than true soul-level sustainability.

The Manifestation Myth

Lack-based Abundance is sold through white-washed visions of quick, American Dream-style success, which promises a shiny future and a picture-perfect life. Meanwhile, camouflaged by motivational jargon and do-good messaging, the modern "manifestation" industry leverages white privilege, beauty privilege, entitlement, and gender hierarchy that contributes to a deeply unequal, discriminatory economic system built on personal feelings of "less than."

In a public dharma talk, a student once asked me about living a life of alignment as a health and wellness industry professional. At the root, I sensed a deep wonder in her question: *How do I manifest a life I love?* Yet I could also hear her need for this to feel "effortless," a desire connected to a glorified idea that Abundance would just click into place if only she could crack the manifestation code.

I responded: *Who said alignment isn't scrappy? Who said alignment isn't filled with painful moments and tough decisions? Who said alignment doesn't mean sacrificing material comforts to invest in yourself in a sustainable way?*

In spiritual spheres, the notion of alignment is connected to a true desire for your professional life to parallel the values of your personal life. And yet, when it gets entangled with the Manifestation Myth—the belief that this should also bring us all the shiny baubles of the American Dream— suddenly we've been duped into believing in an entitled, easy breezy brand of evolution that actually only perpetuates inequality.

The truth? A personal alignment journey is one that may not make sense to anybody else. It won't "feel good" all of the time, nor will it be pleasurable and easy. Manifestation is 99% considered, skillful action. And cultivating skillful action requires a deep upheaval of our entrenched beliefs, great discipline, daily practice, and many energetic trade-offs.

Imagine a marketing email with the headline: *Get Ready for a SHIT STORM! To Rise You Must Let Go of Everything You Cling to for Safety!*

Would you click to purchase?

Instead, the Manifestation Myth headlines feed directly into the Lack/Abundance binary:

Create Your Dream Life in 30 Days (because the life you have sucks)
Manifest a 6-Figure Job You Love (because more money equals more happiness)
Gratitude: The Secret To Success (the more you already have the more you deserve)

These headlines promise change and so-called "growth" to a select few, while doing nothing to address individual feelings of "less than" that lie beneath, or wider issues around inequality. But if we are willing to examine where we have created "Abundance" at the expense of another, we begin to break the binary and move towards a sharing economy, reassigning where we place value, and circulating prana—the renewable fluctuation of vibrant life force—in a radically responsible way that creates the conditions for all of us to grow.

Ask Yourself:

Is my vision of alignment and personal success respectful to the growth and success of others?

Am I putting the work in, day-in and day-out, when no one is watching?

On the deepest energetic level, do I steal from others or hoard resources? (Look closely at relationships: co-workers, mentors/bosses, familial relationships, etc.)

Do I allow the success of another to jeopardize my personal understanding of my own resources?

The truthful and heartfelt answers to these questions will start to illuminate how you might be clinging to The Manifestation Myth.

The Law of Attraction Myth

You will attract abundance when you feel grateful
When you are sharing 'high vibes' you will get high vibes back
Like attracts like

The popular idea of the Law of Attraction reads something like this: "A process of like energy attracts like energy, through which a person can improve their health, wealth, and personal relationships."

This "good vibes only" myth encourages us to replicate what we see as "positive" regardless of its cultural implications. We mimic what we think looks successful, without taking its long-term sustainability or collective repercussions into account, chasing Lack-based Abundance without questioning its morals or methods. Yet if we trap ourselves within the idea that "like attracts like"—for example, that the "richer" we feel the richer we will become—we also buy into an idea of "wealth" that upholds an imbalanced economic and energetic system. This thinking also requires that we mutate our creative force to fit productivity standards. Thus, productivity and creativity become one and the same, and dreaming becomes just another arm of the capitalist machine.

In its purest form, creativity lives outside of the material realm, giving rise to something that does not yet exist. Pure creativity does not replicate, reproduce, mimic or copy; instead, it moves in an imaginative direction that has no desired or fixed outcome.

Ask Yourself:

If you quit your job tomorrow, what would do with the next month? If money was not a limiting factor, how would you spend your days in pure pleasure?

I encourage my students to dream big, yet when faced with big questions like the above, they often stumble. I have seen all kinds of responses to this prompt:

I don't know
This thought is bringing up so much anxiety for me

I think I would run out of things to do
I would worry about how I was going to make money

Even if they have some vague idea, the underpinnings of the Lack/Abundance binary, which equates creativity with productivity, are still present. Through institutional, educational, and inherited fear, the need to fit in, and the shaming of pleasure and play, our dream muscle has atrophied. We no longer know how to dream bigger than the aspirations we have been fed. Many of us move through life never really feeling the innate ecstasy of creation or imagination. This "gap" feels like the boredom and dissatisfaction we try to fill by consuming more "things." Often, imagination quickly mutates into worried "what ifs," fueling states of anxiety and psychic imbalance.

How to Recover? Schedule "Unscheduled Time" DAILY.
Block off 30-60 minutes a day to DO NOTHING. One of my students—a busy entrepreneur and mother—uses a green pen to mark this in her calendar, calling it her "green box time." Your "green box time" is NOT for productive or agenda-based activities, like cleaning, cooking, practicing, helping kids with homework, or even a creative project with an end goal, like sewing a skirt. This time isn't even to be used for meditating, because even then the "aim" for many burnt-out practitioners is a more energetically Abundant end.

Protect this daily unscheduled time fiercely. Resist all urges to overbook this time, or use it for an end goal. Do not watch TV or read during this time. Yes, I am even suggesting you put down this book during this time! Watch yourself and the trickery of the mind. Notice its insatiable, conditioned impulse to slip into productivity. Simply observe yourself being the funny little animal that you are.

PERSONAL INQUIRY PRACTICE:
IDENTIFY YOUR LACK LANDSCAPE

From the ashes
Of egoic burning
Who has the power to
Set a value?
A price?

A worth upon
Humanity
The deepest rumblings
Of self-respect
Rise from the Venusian

Ground within
Where Embodied
Reciprocity between
Concept, Community, and Self-Worth
Ride together

Genuine Abundance is not created through maximum productivity that is motivated from a place of Lack, or panicked attempts to fill what we feel is "missing" with yet more stuff. Instead, it is fostered by adopting a more fluid understanding of equality and symbiotic exchange. To truly break the have/have-not spin cycle and hear this voice of equanimous Abundance within us, we must first visit and confront the landscape of Lack inside of us. These tucked-away Lack lands deplete our discernment and prevent the growth of our imagination—the very tool that will lift us beyond the binary to a place where our deeper needs are actually met.

Take time to experiment with the prompts in this section. Observe what is occurring in your internal and external worlds with a clear, objective eye. Pause each time you sense emptiness in the gut, shakiness in the voice, craving in the belly, or emotional instability in the mind, suspending judgment and coming back to the practice.

And don't forget to tread lightly as you begin to overthrow the personal belief systems that have kept you craving Abundance from the Lack binary. Attempts to get this part "right" will only add weight to what you are ready to overthrow. What the quantum feels and responds to is your effort towards equanimity within the transmission.

Consumerism Inquiry

Begin by evaluating how you consume, and the energy you're sharing with the collective as a result. Ask yourself:

1) *Where in my life do I fall for Lack-marketing as a consumer?* Look closely at the products you buy, and the ideals behind your purchases. Write this out in detail, highlighting your motivation narrative. Get honest: if your answer is "I needed it," why was this?

2) *Am I aware of the chain of production behind what I consume?* Pick several products or services to examine and research. Can you estimate how many beings contributed to your consumption of this product or service? Did it cause violence in any ecosystem as it came into being? Can you take a moment to honor and thank all of the causes and conditions that gave you access to consume these things?

3) *What sort of egoic "hit" did you receive from the purchase?* What part of your ego received praise, a boost, or validation for purchasing that product or service?

4) *In the end, did you play directly into your Lack mentality in making this purchase?* For example, did you go on a massive price hunt extravaganza with the mindset that "the less I spend, the more Abundance for me?" What were all the energetic trades (your time, others' labor, the Earth's resources etc.) at play in this? I'm not advocating for spending beyond your means here, but simply for committing to looking more deeply at where you are attached to Lack.

Self-Worth and Lack-Wound Inquiry

Use these questions to identify the deeper motivations behind consuming and sharing your personal resources, highlighting when you reach outside of yourself because of a personal Lack-wound or damaged sense of self-worth.

1) *What steps do I take to rejuvenate my own energetic reserves, every single day?* When we don't clearly outline these personal steps, we keep social engagements and hold onto imbalanced friend relationships that drain our energy, and burn out on too much tech time.

2) *To what extent do I covet the lives of others, ignoring my own life's teachings?* When we put another person on a pedestal or wish for our own lives to be different, we immediately devalue ourselves and therefore act from the Lack side of the binary.

3) *Do I have thoughts of self-hatred and self-judgment?* Allowing these kinds of thoughts to replay in our minds contributes to an embodied state of Lack over time. Write them out in detail and do not allow them to fester in the darkness of your mind.

4) *What energetic trade did I make to bring that product, service, person, place or thing into my life?* Every decision we make with our resources is a trade. What human resources did you give up in order to bring that new thing into your life? Did you devalue your own time or energy in the process of this trade?

Creativity Inquiry

Reflecting on the below questions will help you realize when your addiction to productivity blocks your creativity. Support this exploration with your "green box time," creating daily space to simply sit with your true nature. Have fun with your answers, take your time, and use your imagination.

1) *To what extent do I rush projects?* Am I more committed to meeting a

deadline than the process itself?

2) *Do I often seek inspiration from outside of myself, attempting to mimic or copy? Why?*

3) *Whose voice is it telling me that my ideas aren't good enough, creative enough, or spiritual enough?*

4) *What excites me?* What feels pleasurable? What is my personal understanding of beauty?

Resource Value Refinement Inquiry

We often devalue resources within ourselves unknowingly, causing us to project our Lack outward and get upset when another person or entity won't share that same resource with us.

Start by noticing these types of thoughts:

It won't take them any time, why can't they just help me?

They have so much money, they can take the hit and loan me some

She has done this before, why can't she just tell me what to do?

There is so much here, I will just take a little—no one will notice

Then, look closely at the following questions and begin to refine your relationship to your own personal resources:

Do I steal time from others? Do I steal knowledge from others?

Do I covet another's grit, but shy away from doing the work in my own life?
Do I dismiss others' hard work by making unfair assumptions about them? (They "had it easy," "got a leg-up," or "don't have the same issues as me.")

Do I steal resources from the Earth?

For this last one, make a list and evaluate your overuse of the Earth's physical resources. Examples include your power usage, fast fashion consumption, food consumption, your relationship to "stuff," and anywhere you take more than you need.

BREAKING THE BINARY: PRANIC ECONOMY

If we really want to uncover how we imprison ourselves and each other in an economy that perpetuates the Lack/Abundance binary, we can't just coast on the surface and work on filling our "gratitude journal." I'll start by asking what might be a triggering question:

If a person, company, or organization generates what appears to be Abundance within our current paradigm, but produces suffering and Lack for others, was Abundance really created?

From a yogic understanding of prana, what was actually perpetuated as the dollars accumulated in the bank was *Lack*. In binary worldview, "success" is often dependent on acquiring wealth without a consideration of our essential needs, the limited time we spend in a human body, or the long-term impacts on our personal and earthly resources and creativity. By not properly valuing these resources, we have caused a rupture in the healthy operation of our economic ecosystem, our overall quality of life, and the radiance of being.

Each day that we continue to operate within our current Lack/Abundance binary moves us deeper into barren landscapes of Lack, and forces us into so-called "expansions" that actually result in insurmountable levels of depletion. The projected result of this collective trajectory? A snuffing out of all human uniqueness and creativity, and a stripping of the Earth's natural beauty.

But before we descend into a dark and gloomy future ...

Enter the Pranic Economy!

The contemplative work of constructing a Pranic Economy means no longer viewing Lack and Abundance on opposite ends of a spectrum. Instead, this new paradigm positions us as vibrational beings that transmit equality and objectivity in the way we share resources with one another.

The Human and Earthly Resources that make up a Pranic Economy are:

Time
Grit or Know-How
Creativity
Money
Emotional Support and Empathy
Earth's Limited Environmental Resources
Community and Well-being

Participating in the Pranic Economy asks you to extend your understanding of resources beyond the exchange of money, goods, and services, and to begin viewing "capital" in a different way—honoring the intrinsic value of the Human and Earthly Resources that have been devalued in our current paradigm.

Start by taking your Pranic Inventory

The demands of each day ask us to be many different people and perform many different roles. Taking inventory on an energetic level helps us identify where we're responding from a place of Lack versus where we're delegating from the seat of Abundance. A Pranic Inventory is best undertaken in the morning or the evening, before or after a long work day. Practice engaging with these questions at least two to three times per week:

Where and with whom do I spend my days? What do I spend them doing?

What feels exhausting for the system? What feels rejuvenating for the system?

Do I feel as though my actions and the actions of those around me contribute to a state of reciprocity?

And the deepest, most transformative question to ask yourself:

How "expensive" was that? Taking into account all the Pranic resources listed above, did you exit the situation feeling net-positive or net-negative, energetically speaking?

These questions have very little to do with cash flow or productivity, but instead pertain to human resources of time, energy, creativity, emotional intelligence, and love. By taking this inventory, you'll start to learn how to truly value yourself, leaving both the Lack-wound and concepts of imbalanced self-serving Abundance behind.

Your Human and Earthly Resources Report
The Pranic Economy is based on moving away from "me, myself, and I" ideas about Abundance, and walking toward a sharing economy that honors self, others, and the collective cultural organization. Creating your own "Human and Earthly Resources Report" will help you shift your worldview by recategorizing how you attribute value to certain resources. Over time, doing this deep upheaval in our personal narratives has the power to change the collective ethos, creating dramatically different, more ethical, social structures of exchange.

Check in with each of these Human and Earthly Resources daily or weekly:

Time: My most limited human resource

Did I use it responsibly today? How will I use it responsibly tomorrow?

Using time responsibly means staying out of fear and leaving anxiety behind. Examples of "irresponsible" uses of time include gossiping, complaining, criticizing, and dwelling on destructive emotions, thereby perpetuating the Lack-wound.

Grit or Know-How: My most precious skill or learning

Did I problem solve with grace today?

Or did you spend most of your day in self-created stress mentality? Tell yourself: If I didn't find an answer, that's okay. I will need resources to keep looking.

Creativity: My innate state of being

Did I give my mind space to dream? Did I have a few moments of feeling boundless today?

Did you partake in a practice, ritual, or activity that was agendaless, for the sole purpose of feeling boundlessly connected to source?

Money: Something I gather and something I share

What went in and what went out? Did I cultivate a reactionless neutrality around this flux?

Within a Pranic Economy, the "idea" of money no longer holds power over our psyches. As we begin to demystify it, we cultivate a reactionless state of neutrality towards its comings and goings.

Emotional Support and Empathy: My understanding of us as all equal

In my actions today, did I express emotional support and honor my own needs? Do I have enough energy to extend heartfelt empathy to those around me?

True empathy means we hold space for what we need without pushing the person or situation or demanding a certain type of behavior.

Earth's Limited Environmental Resources: My commitment to being a responsible consumer

Did I consume with care and attention? Did I share resources with openness?

Valuing the Earth's resources means we are responsible with how and what we consume. Keeping this cycle of give and take in balance allows us to consume sustainably and share freely, in both spiritual and material ways.

Community and Well-being: I am only as healthy as the world around me

Did my actions in my personal and professional life contribute to energetic sustainability in my community?

Becoming aware of the entire Pranic ecosystem that supports us means reflecting on and acknowledging all of the causes and conditions that both preceded and will follow our actions, to the best of our ability.

Reflecting Upon Each of These Human and Earthly Resources, Truly Ask Yourself:

Which ones are topped off, and which feel barren?

Is my way of life sustainable in all of these areas?

And then, start to take it even further by asking:

Instead of selling or purchasing from a place of deep-seated Lack, am I selling and purchasing while taking the full health of the ecosystem into account?

I can hear your mind now, responding: What if I don't have enough money to buy the more expensive organic option? I don't even value my own time, how can I value others' time? I have three kids to feed—I don't have enough for us, let alone anything left to share. I have rent to pay and healthcare to purchase so I have to work all the time.

Yes, yes, and yes! Precisely. Dig it all up. Noticing these Lack-based thought-forms reminds us that replacing them with cheesy law of attraction "I receive what I believe" vibes isn't enough. Instead, we must do the deep work that the Pranic Economy asks of us, which means uprooting harmful definitions of commerce and capital, and revaluing our Human and Earthly Resources. This is the only way to dismantle the current Lack/Abundance binary and step out into a space of true "enoughness."

As you practice taking your Pranic Inventory and creating your Human and Earthly Resources Report, you'll notice that your values, self-identity, and relationships will begin to shift. Stay tuned for these types of thought evolutions:

I have more than enough for me and my family.

I don't need to hoard wealth to fill my Lack-wound. Instead, I share wealth with many.

I would be happy to support you in your journey of creation—my resources are very high right now.

I take only what I need. If I take more, I am taking from others who might actually need this more than me.

Not everyone on Earth values their personal resources like I value mine. What actions can I take to lighten the load on the collective and on the Earth?

This relationship cycle (personal or professional) has run its course, and I am prepared to let it go with ease. I do not feel "less than" watching it come to an end. In fact I feel prosperous, trusting that something else is on the horizon.

Genuine Abundance is a state of being. When I value my human resources and the sustainable use of earthly resources, this is reflected back by my surroundings.

SUBTLE BODY PRACTICE
Adapting to Change with Ease Meditation

All of the exercises in the preceding sections have worked to rearrange our consciousness in waking life. Now, we're ready to dive even deeper, dismantling our attachment to the Lack/Abundance binary on a subconscious level. Our subconscious is like the tectonic plates beneath the intellectual crust, and meditative practice shifts this subconscious programming. By bringing our subtle body (auric energy and biofield) into alignment through practice, we affect thought-form organization in our conscious, waking lives. We begin to cultivate an embodied understanding of our own Human and Earthly Resources that is aligned with Pranic Economic values, adapting to change with ease. This is the precursor to flowstate (which will come into play in the Fifth Binary: Hustle/Flow). We'll bring our transcendence of the Lack/Abundance binary into an embodied state of realization.

This breath pattern and mantra are designed to create settling and safety in the system, excavating thought-forms connected to the Lack wound and circulating creativity by relaxing self-created stress. To be imaginative, we must learn to rest in a receptive state. Let's practice together.

Posture
Sit in Sukhasana, or a simple, cross-legged seat. Prop yourself, if necessary, to support your body. Make this easy on your posture and feel free to lean against something. If knee pain is present, you can always straighten your legs and support your lower back, or sit in a chair.

Mudra
Gyan mudra—thumb and Jupiter finger (index finger) are touching. We have been here before, and for good reason, as this is a "Maha mudra": a great or grand mudra that spans across many traditions. It is also discreet and powerful and you can feel free to use it at any point during the day to train your attention.

Breath Pattern

Breathe in through the nose out through the mouth, in through the mouth, out through the nose. Repeat this breath pattern for the duration of the meditation. You don't have to set out to practice this at any particular speed; your pace will change in duration and from day to day. Pay attention to these fluctuations. Chances are if you are trying to shake the binary thinking that's motivated by Lack from your day, a rapid pattern might be present. Watch how it changes with focus and relaxation, as you cultivate a greater sense of safety. Generally the more time you spend bringing awareness to your breath the more stable, and less erratic, it becomes over time. All of this breath pattern intel reveals your inner state. Also pay close attention to the amount of time it takes for you to "drop-in," which is meditator code for that moment when you "stop doing, and allow."

Mantra on Breath Rhythm

Phenomena arises (in through the nose)

Phenomena distingrates (out through the mouth)

I gather resources (in through the mouth)

I share resources (out through the nose)

Repeat the mantra mentally for several rounds as you enter into the landscape of your meta-dialogue and inner reality. It's totally alright if the words fall away after several rounds of recitation. If the mind is extra bouncy on certain days, use these four lines to slow and focus the attention.

Timing

Practice for a minimum of 11 minutes daily for 30+ consecutive days.

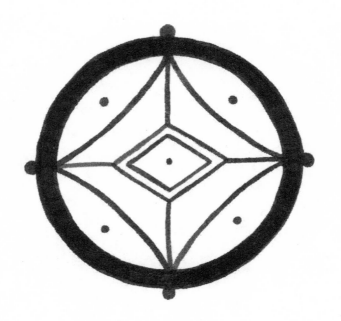

THE FIFTH BINARY
HUSTLE/FLOW: ELEVATED CAPACITY

Beth, a very creative and fiery long-term student of mine, possessed a quick mind, confidence, and competence that pushed her towards constant creation. A super mom who was academically decorated, with a full-time job and several side hustles, Beth was bubbly, always giving, and truly brilliant to converse with, filling the role of "ideas girl" in many social situations.

But when you slowed her down and asked her how she was doing, her posture would relax from a hardened pride in her chest to a heavy slump. The truth of her inner state was that she often felt downright exhausted. For years, she had been pushing herself to the point where she felt completely *spent*. The same fiery aspects of Beth's personality that fueled her creativity had gotten co-opted by binary worldview's over-productive "Hustle." With professional demands that dismissed her soft humanness and shackled her to a life of overexertion, she had become addicted to the "mover and shaker" opportunities that this overexertion brought her way. The voice of her Hustle said "yes" to it all—seeking another hit for her ego's addiction to feeling needed, important, and successful. She had also come to mistake being "busy" for an abundant flowstate, and wondered why nothing actually felt fluid.

When she tried to slow down, she felt guilty for not dedicating her downtime to doing activities with her kids. If she stepped off the hamster wheel at work, she feared that others would think she wasn't living up to her potential, or that her project was a flop. No matter how hard Beth tried, she could not hustle her way to the flowstate she desired—one built on sustainable values, and a joyous, contented connection between head and heart. Her desperate attempts to reach Flow as an "outcome" of Hustle were leading to a tsunami of spiritual bypassing and an ever-elusive search for true body/mind equilibrium.

Even her spiritual practice had become entangled with her Hustle. When I suggested that she try skipping her morning sadhana, Beth found she was so wed to the idea that "slacking" meant failure, that she couldn't quit waking up at 5am to squeeze it in. Her practice had become yet another item on her to-do list: an accolade for the ego instead of a transformative act of sacred self-care.

If Beth's story is familiar to you, it's because a binary worldview that's fueled by capitalist values has left many of us addicted to the Hustle; while at the other end of the binary, we idealize and crave being able to "relax" into Flow. The internal script goes something like:

If things aren't working, it's my job to work harder

If I get up earlier I'll be able to do more with my day

I need a deadline to get anything done

If I work hard today, I will earn myself time to relax

The addiction to a "busy" life that associates productivity with tangible "results" in the material realm is a key sign of being trapped in the Hustle/Flow binary. This binary tells us that productivity is built from a painful, uphill, triumphant Hustle that requires us to do more and more with busy bodies that are always working. We push to produce, monetize, and expand.

The cheap idea that fuels this endless Hustle? That we can do it all and have it all!

The cold hard truth? No, we can't.

The Hustle/Flow binary constantly tells us that busier always equals better, while dangling the cosmic carrot that once we have achieved and attained a certain level of "success," the work part will become easier or nonexistent. Within this worldview, "making it" becomes a greedily gainful way out, concerned with amassing more resources so we can finally quit working and relax. Caught up in the Hustle/Flow binary, we either mistake being busy and constantly saying "yes" as Flow, or we position Flow as the elusive reward for all this endless and exhausting Hustle. We may find ourselves thinking:

I need to start putting myself first

I need to step-up my self-care

As modern technology enables ever-increasing levels of Hustle, we've been led to believe that the cure for burnout and depletion simply rests in better time management or "slowing down." Yet this thinking actually further ensnares us in the Hustle/Flow binary, where productivity and self-image are also linked. We find ourselves turning to every trendy quick fix under the sun, from apps to healing circles to calming oils, which only end up lengthening our to-do lists. Flow becomes just another concept to strive for—adding to our energetic commitments rather than helping us reorganize them.

Many of us also seek to embrace Flow by flouting all sense of structure. Our voice becomes meek, our personal standards become too watery, and all of a sudden we aren't getting much done. We have quietly faded into the backdrop of mediocre apathy. This too is an easy place to spiritually bypass, and we hear this often in language that sounds like:

Oh man, I don't know, I am just going with the flow

I had to help this person, and do this, so I never actually got to it

I am not sure what to do, or how to start; I'm going to wait for Spirit to show me the way

While true flowstate is not something that can be attained through over-effort or greed, nor can it be attained by apathetically "leaning out" and letting life happen to us. The flowstate we desire as a counter to the Hustle/Flow binary arises from a quiet mind, and it is catalyzed through open, unrushed, receptive, and intuitive states of being. This is not the "sitting around and meditating by the river" cartoon version of contentment, but a backdrop of resilient, stable contentment that motivates engaged action.

So how do we break this cycle?

We start by shifting our definitions of work, productivity, and success, based on the understanding that all resources are limited (as discussed in relation to the Lack/Abundance binary)—including our self and time. From here, we start to create different boundaries around the use of our energy, skillfully applying our attention and discernment to tap into a "healthy" Hustle that swaps the endless slog of "work" for an ethically sustainable vision of service.

Flow naturally informs and becomes the backdrop for this healthy Hustle, as we connect to a personal, intuitive rhythm that's unique to us— not an end goal, but a moment-by-moment intuitive navigation that informs how we make decisions and use our energy. In contrast to the Hustle/Flow binary, this version of service actually recharges the one doing the work; work gets done all while flowstate stays intact. We shift from an oppressive system of overproduction and self-sacrifice to a backdrop of contentment that prizes personal agency and intuitive connection.

In this chapter, we'll look deeply at the social structures and personal belief systems that fuel the overworking and undermining of self that have so tightly bound us to the always-sinking ship of Hustle. We will also examine how we came to idealize Flow as a static end state to attain, thereby separating us from personal agency and moment-by-moment connection to our intuitive navigation. In doing so, we'll swap the burnout cycle for good, dismantling our notions of "pushing it hard" to reconnect to our "Elevated Capacity," based on attention, intuition, and energy regulation.

THE MYTHS OF HUSTLE/FLOW

The Harder Is Better Myth

From early on, we are taught that success is the result of hard work, and lots of it. In this context, our definitions of "work" and "success" are often based on linear thinking—the idea that if I perform X, I will achieve Y— and narrow ideas of what it means to "be somebody" in the world. The threat of punishment for failing or falling out of line is also established in childhood, and follows us into adulthood. We learn to do work in a specific way and to do what we are told, without question, or else risk social rejection and economic hardship.

In the process, we lose more and more of our personal agency and connection to our intuition. The pressures of work, compounded by the depletion of overworking and feelings of purposelessness resulting from us following a societally-approved path to success that may have nothing to do with our personal desires, lead us to a state of burnout. And yet the only "solution" we have is to Hustle harder and keep reaching outside of ourselves to attain an end goal.

Inside our extractive capitalistic system, material worth often gets confused for self-worth; and attaching our value as people to the value of our output is where we can get "addicted" to the Hustle. We never feel "good enough" because we never "have/achieve" enough. And within a global society that's increasingly more dependent on technology, pushing our very humanity to keep up with "productivity" is a zero-sum game.

It is crucial that we examine the cultural subliminal messaging around "success," reclaim it, and separate our intrinsic self-worth from a manufactured dream of success that keeps us powerless and obedient—forever pushing to attain an elusive "something" within a system of endless extraction.

Let's unpack where we might have mistakenly mixed up our self-worth with manufactured versions of success:

What is "Success" for Me?

Begin by exploring your own concept of "work" and the Hustle hooks that keep you striving for "success" to the point of exhaustion.

Give each of the questions and their subtext time for in-depth reflection—these are the flashing neon signs that keep you attached to the Hustle/Flow binary that leads toward burnout.

1) *How is my self-worth bolstered by my addiction to Hustle?* We all want to feel "accomplished" and there's nothing wrong with that. But dig deeper and be precise: do you feel more worthy when you are busier? Why?

2) *In what situations in my life do I overwork, sacrificing my own well-being?* Write these situations out in detail. Take note of when you continually override or ignore your intuition in certain situations and just keep working—this is how you'll uncover where you swap self-trust for self-sacrifice.

3) *How has "conventional success" been defined within my psyche?* Clearly outline jobs, partners, moves, or cities that you chose to fit the picture of "making it," but which ultimately let you down because of the disconnect between this conventional image and your own intuitive knowing.

4) *What professional environments and relationships am I ready to leave behind, because they demand I overwork at the expense of self?* Imagine that your new worldview is: I CANNOT DO IT ALL. With this in mind, take inventory of your life and begin to determine the people, places and environments to which you are ready to rescind your energetic commitments.

5) *If I choose to rest, to say NO, and to step away from Hustle, what are the common emotions that arise?* Saying NO might bring up shame, failure, self-judgment, and comparison, because it is the first time in many relationships you have chosen to honor yourself—both turning

your back on Hustle and forgoing an overly flexible Flow to accommodate others. When we initiate mega change in our lives, we have to know that we've got our own backs. And to do this, self-punishment has got to go.

The Magic Bullet Myth

Raise your hand if you have ever found yourself making this kind of a commitment to tending to your "well-being":

I am going to wake up with the rising sun, and start with a freezing cold shower. Then I will write my goal-setting journal entry in front of the blue light, followed by my keto-adaptogen smoothie, with a side of grass-fed butter coffee. Outside of work, I have to make time for my vit-C drip appointment and then rush to my acupuncture sesh this evening.

The long list of hacks and self-care solutions goes on, as if our bodies and minds can be rushed into flowstate. The promise of the "magic pill" that's going to flip the script pushes us to bombard our systems with what the wellness industry deems as "good stimulus" and to treat our healing journey like just another job. We see this glorified Hustle operating at all levels: from personal beliefs like Beth's self-justifying need to complete morning sadhana to get her gold star, to the wellness industry's self-gratifying race to "get the edge" by discovering the latest product or technique that's going to result in optimal health or spiritual enlightenment.

Do many of these products feel good? Oh yes!

Do they potentially increase health and bio-markers? Yes indeed

BUT

Do they do anything to dismantle the underlying belief that busy is better? No

Do they prevent you from over-working, depletion, and burning out? No

Trust me, my intellectual mind loves reading new studies, trying new products, and experimenting with my own body/mind. Transcending this binary is not about developing a worldview rooted in absolutes, but about introducing new habits with awareness and a commitment to reorganizing our Hustle addiction. The process of reorganizing our self-care routine so that it truly supports our healthy Hustle and our intuitive Flow begins with another critical question: *Am I reaching outside of myself to attain something that is actually available on the inside?*

No matter how "conscious" our wellness choices, they still often find us reaching outside of ourselves for solutions instead of looking inwards towards the divine organization of our own energetic systems. Sustainable flowstate is a quality of mind that responds with equilibrium to our constantly changing bodies and surrounding physical circumstances. The secret? We don't have to go anywhere, move anything, or add anything to regain our energetic equilibrium.

Use this exercise to look at how your addiction to Hustle might co-opt your attempts at authentic well-being. Examine the inner motivations behind your behaviors and get real with yourself!

1) *Am I hiding my addiction to Hustle in spiritual language or wellness purchases?* Addiction to Hustle shows up in many ways that culture deems healthy and unhealthy; look closely at both ends of the spectrum. For example, we might even hide our Hustle addiction in an obsession with fitness, disordered eating that we call "healthy," seeking certification after certification, or adding preposterous amounts of products to our routine in pursuit of lifestyle perfection. The list goes on. Be honest with yourself and also examine what society deems "healthy" practices, checking how you might be hiding Hustle in those avenues too.

2) *Is my attachment to wellness trends stopping me from doing the authentic inner work?* You'll know this is happening when you perform a Google search or try a new product every time something feels "off." Or instead of sitting with the intensity of organic transformation, you

try to take control with performative public acts to reassure your egoic identity, "you are doing the right thing."

3) *Do I make time to deeply contemplate and sit with the complexity of my own suffering?* Granted, this doesn't sound like fun. But when you keep succumbing to the "upsell," thinking that the next new teaching or course will finally give you clarity, you are bypassing what your body and your psyche have to say to you. Develop a healthy line of inner inquiry that plays devil's advocate in your meta-dialogue and is always willing to challenge thoughts we attach to very quickly.

Look carefully at where you reach outside of yourself for access to flow-state or avoid taking personal responsibility. It is not the practice or product we reach for that is the issue, but the constant state of grasping for a solution. This simply produces more Hustle—leading to more chaotic energy, longer to-do lists, and neglect for the quiet spaces where we can begin to regain our personal agency. This is precisely where we find a contented "backdrop" flowstate that's not fiercely fought for or rewarded as the end goal of Hustle, but is borne out of moment-by-moment intuitive decision-making that honors what best contributes to our unique, and ever-changing, sense of well-being.

The Because I've Earned It Myth
Hard work always pays off
Eat your veggies and you'll get dessert
Treat yourself; you deserve it (said after a grueling day at the office or sweaty workout)

In professional, personal, and spiritual contexts, we're often told that the "payoff" is coming somewhere in a distant future: the promotion after endless overtime; the perfect partner after exhausting self-work; or the earth-shaking "awakening" after years of spiritual practice. We're told that if we just "stick with" any current discomfort, we'll eventually be rewarded with something extra sweet in the end.

The idea behind this myth is that the end goal and accomplishment make the "bad parts" along the way somehow worth it; that suffering somehow makes our "success" sweeter. But while some degree of discomfort is inevitable in the evolutionary process, this myth encourages a misaligned Hustle mentality that positions Flow as a glossy reward that we'll finally receive after years of suffering—much of it unnecessary and borne out of our addiction to busyness. The result is that we become addicted to the unnecessary discomfort of endless Hustle, and come to see Flow as an end goal rather than a creative and playful state that's available to us in any moment.

As in the Magic Bullet Myth, where Flow ends up as part of our Hustle, here we end up trying to Hustle our way to Flow. But flowstate doesn't arise from the fake it till you make it approach; instead, this approach actually causes further damage by training the central nervous system to recognize "agitation" as progress. This keeps us stuck swinging between the idea that "work" equals "hard" Hustle, and that the enjoyment and pleasure of "play" can only be found after we've put in the effort to get out the reward. This "dessert after veggies" mentality damages our ability to break the work/play binary, and thus to uncover creativity, curiosity, and play in a great variety of situations.

We end up endlessly fueling a system that runs on an auto-pilot valuation of Hustle, and never learn the patterns and skills that bring about true ease—and a new way to value the entire process that's not just about the payoff of the "earned" end goal. Ease is a precursor to flowstate, and central nervous system regulation happens throughout the entire process of creation—from start to finish—not just at the so-called "end." A previous teacher of mine shared the following with me in a dharma talk:

"You want the newest coolest thing. So you work your ass off saving the money, taking on extra shifts, projects or clients. You spread yourself so thin during the process of trying to attain the best, new coolest thing." Alternately, "Someone just hands you this newest coolest thing. You are content for about a split second. Even though you now possess the newest coolest thing."

So why does your contentment only last for a few fleeting seconds? Because it was never the newest, coolest thing that you actually wanted, even though your mind told you that for weeks, months, years. Instead, you were deeply attached to the wanting: the desire that drove your misaligned Hustle, and seemingly gave you and all your hard work a "purpose." In reality, this process had little to do with "getting" the object and everything to do with justifying your misaligned Hustle; an upregulated central nervous system—sparked through over-working—was the only thing your body/mind was registering as valuable or purposeful. So you reach the end goal, get the thing, and then the subconscious process begins all over again.

To break the input-output feedback loop of putting in endless Hustle to "achieve" elusive Flow, we must start to explore the self-created ways we cause suffering, and commit to uncovering a flowstate that comes from cultivating ease in the process. We can do this by starting to ask bigger questions like:

Why does this have to be so hard? Is there anything in my control that I can change?

Why do I put up with this level of pressure from our extractive capitalist economy? Is there anything I can say NO to?

What is it within me that prevents me from perceiving an outcome's value that isn't tied to the struggle to get there?

How can I start calling in more ease along the way?

How would creating more ease in my body and simplicity in my mindset start to change the entire process of attaining a goal? And how might my goals themselves start to shift as well?

PERSONAL INQUIRY PRACTICE: IDENTIFY ABUSE OF INTENSITY

Beyond the illusion
Of Work/Reward
There lies
My resting
Second Nature

No Need to Push
To Strive, to Cling
For that scares
Creativity, its soft body
Becomes illusive

In all that hardness
The more we "work"
For it
We forget how to
Uncover it

When it's channeled into the right activities, intensity—which we associate with the engaged aliveness of Hustle—is a beautiful thing. But when it's exploited and misused, we end up with competitive, loose cannon energy that fuels violence towards the self, and bolsters the "push harder" narrative of the Hustle/Flow binary.

We all have a personal pattern of misplaced intensity, often cultivated in the younger years spent chasing good grades, engaging in competitive sports, or some other manifestation of the narrative that we must "be the best." We often harbor unconscious grief, shame, and resentment about this early exploitation of our natural healthy Hustle. As a result, aggression and competition ooze into our adult lives, as we become addicted to moving up the corporate ladder or obsessed with pick-up soccer leagues and ultra-running. You name it.

Meanwhile, we avoid stillness at all costs, seeing it as a "waste of time." When we run out of work or sporting activities to channel our excess of intensity, we instead turn to substances, or dramatic, emotionally charged relationships. The urge to compete, "be known," and receive praise has grown so large that it dominates all areas of our lives. Before we know it, we have spent all our Hustle this way, and find ourselves running on empty.

Moving beyond the Hustle/Flow binary also means gathering up and repurposing this fiery energy, so that we can put it into the things we feel truly passionate about. To do this, we must engage in some mindful excavation of our personal story of misaligned Hustle, competition, and comparison, which will help us identify where and how our striving for "success" is actually leading to suffering and self-abuse.

Each one of the prompts in the exercise below is meant to evoke a memory. Approach this inquiry with a sense of levity and creativity. You're not meant to answer these questions as if you were taking a high school test. Instead, playfully explore placing yourself back in the memory, giving voice to the intuitive, self-aware side of you that didn't have space to speak in the past. Write your memories out in detail: what you were wearing, where you were standing—really describe the scene. Then, describe the energetic context of the scene: how you felt, the emotional verbiage that was exchanged. If the memories don't come through right away, no big deal. Simply move on to the next question and come back with fresh eyes when the memory presents itself. The juice lies in looking at your emotional response. How did this moment affect your perception of self? How long have you been replaying this idea in your adult life as if it were still truth?

It's time to excavate the archetypes within our psyches that are causing misplaced intensity and keeping us addicted to Hustle:

1) *Pull out the parental narratives lodged in the psyche.* How did your parents feel about work? Can you remember what it was like to observe this as a child? Describe the scene, the words they used, your mood, and how their emotional understanding of work did or didn't transfer to you.

2) *Recall a time in childhood when homework, schoolwork, or extracurricular*

work felt like a chore, a hassle, or a competition to your playful conscious-ness. Transport yourself to the scene, the pencil you were holding, the overalls you were wearing. Using your creativity, truly recall as many details as possible.

3) *Reflect on a time when you "failed" in school.* What was the punishment like; what sort of narrative did this develop in your mindstream moving forward? What was the mood and the posture of your young body as you experienced the perceived failure and its fall-out? How did it feel as you started to experience this neurocircuitry of overwhelm?

4) *Write about a moment more recently where you were trapped in the self-di-minishing game of comparison.* Whether it was while scrolling on so-cial media or hearing about someone else's success, highlight the key emotions and, more importantly, anything that was triggered in your mindstream about how you might personally "do better" or "get ahead." Put yourself right back in that moment, describing the setting and exactly how it felt.

5) *If you could take a snapshot of personal fulfillment in your day-to-day, de-scribe what that scene would look like.* What are your duties? What does creative personal time look like? How do you seek pleasure daily?

6) *Examine any addictions to "getting the edge," and competitive thought patterns in your psyche, and describe in detail how you use this narrative to engage in self-abuse.* Illustrate the exact thoughts you fall back on when you feel like you are "falling short" or not keeping up with over-production, noticing where excessive time management puts you in competition with yourself, and with time itself.

Let each of these prompts live like short stories about your past, showing how addiction to Hustle and competition was built over time. The pro-foundly personal experiences and answers to these questions will illuminate behavioral patterns that are playing on a loop and deepening your addiction to Hustle.

Resist the urge to speak discursively and describe the setting and deeply-felt emotion instead. This is where the intel lies—what comes up speaks greatly to our held beliefs, emotional attachments, and the layers of conditioned behavior. Some aspects of the past will be surprising, and memory is not a fool-proof technology. That is why I am asking you to get creative and read between the lines of your artistic expression. As you immerse yourself in these memories, the answers to these questions will start to illuminate all the ways you are staying attached to the Hustle and denying yourself access to true flowstate. Give them the time and attention they deserve. The cultivation of attention is the first step towards healing our Hustle, as we learn to more carefully regulate our intensity and personal life force.

BREAKING THE BINARY: ELEVATED CAPACITY

Now that we've excavated our roadblocks to sustainable flowstate by drawing our Hustle addiction to the surface, it's time to repurpose our energy and begin to cultivate what I call "Elevated Capacity." Hang in there with me during this section; it takes a different quality of mind to reach Elevated Capacity, which utilizes a completely different skill set than the usual "pushing" and "figuring out" associated with the Hustle/Flow binary.

According to the tenets of Elevated Capacity, output is not based on "how much I do" but on having a clear, unhurried worldview of what actually needs to be done, and how to do it. Since all stress is self-created, less frivolous mental input can create more powerful energetic output. Meanwhile, flowstate is not something to achieve or to "hack"—it is a way of being that is the natural byproduct of aligned action.

Elevated Capacity is built upon a very simple concept of "right action," as referenced in several Buddhist lineages. In fact, the concept is so simple that our minds, and our work-addicted culture, like to create confusion around it. As the antidote to the Hustle/Flow binary, Elevated Capacity is part of a new paradigm where there is no place to go, no state of being to chase. Rather, "right action" is the means to an end in and of it-self—a creative process of accumulated skillful actions that have the power to create a personal sense of well-being and contentment that is unique to us. In the previous sections, we looked at the "unskillful actions" that have been attached to old paradigms of work and success. And now we're ready to focus on the "skillful actions" that will help us align naturally with our flow.

Expanding our Elevated Capacity asks us to develop three qualities: Attention, Intuitive Efficiency, and Proper Energy Use. I define these as:

Attention: Undivided focus on your inner motivations, intentions, and personal trickery. Truly contemplating the ways your actions and speech have sought to enhance misaligned Hustle, and exploring your addiction to asserting yourself in a way that is outdated and related to past concepts of oppressive success.

Intuitive Efficiency: A higher level of mind that can be applied to taking actions that align with our personal definition of success. Guidance that is no longer contaminated by motivations to protect an identity that hides in the Hustle—based on busyness, being the "best," or "having it all."

Proper Energy Use: Now, personal contemplative attention is activated in daily life, and intuition becomes the motivator of action itself. In this shift, misaligned Hustle begins to feel like a waste of energy. We learn to stop over-efforting and to start cultivating sustainable, present moment "right action" with our energy. Managing our energy with clarity means we're not obsessed with anyone else's definition of success or work. It means breaking up with binary visions of multitasking and "getting it done" and the self-created stress of trying to meet those standards.

By engaging these three qualities, interfacing with the misaligned Hustle no longer feels like a weight. Now, our attention is as sharp as a knife, our intuition cuts through misperceptions about what it means to "achieve," and proper energy use reorganizes our thought forms and actions moment-by-moment, laying the yellow brick road of flowstate.

Sound more sustainable? Let's get started ...

Practices for Attention

It is a common spiritual saying that "everything is a teaching." Well then, in all seriousness, why aren't we treating our daily lives with the respect they deserve—closely examining our self-created stress, burnout, and fired-up nervous systems as actual teachings?

1) *Examine your own self-created stress with hyper-objective scrutiny.* This will by no means be a comfortable inquiry. We must take full responsibility for all misperceptions that lead to dysregulated life force use. Think back to the opening section of this binary, and use Beth's layered actions as jumping off points in your own meta-dialogue. Did any of those behaviors feel familiar? Clearly write out your personal context of self-created stress.

2) *Where are the stickiest points of emotional attachment in my "work life"?* Write this out in detail: the people, situations, co-workers, and organizations that have caused you deep emotional and psychological pain. This process might be complicated, and it might be very simple—trust where your attention goes as you sort through this emotional minefield.

3) *How have you protected this emotional attachment?* We often find ways to bypass the self-created stress narrative we project onto many people, places, and things. Use your attention to dig into this story, looking at anywhere you make yourself "right" with defensiveness, or quickly shift your attention to toxic positivity in order to bypass challenges and focus on the things you do well.

Practices for Intuitive Efficiency

By "normal" societal standards, intuition is labelled "witchy," "spiritual" or "prophetic." But to the yogi, intuition is simply a potent byproduct of the practice. Cultivating our intuition in our day-to-day connects us to higher octaves of consciousness that are often trampled on by Hustle addiction. With Intuitive Efficiency, we tap into a new kind of doing, dwelling in the headspace of creation that is not tightly bound to overproduction, while making healing connections between ourselves and our community.

1) *Don't go seeking—practice LISTENING.* Intuition has a voice of its own that is unmistakable. It has a very different tone than "I should do this because ..." Instead, intuition is less prescriptive and more expansive, speaking to each one of us differently through states of embodiment—whether it's visions, sounds, gut knowings, or other methods entirely. Cultivating your attention, as per the previous practices, will allow you to tune in to its subtle language.

2) *An important promise to self: do not share how your intuition sounds with others.* Connecting to your intuition is a personal process and you're asked to respect this relationship. Broadcasting its sacred sound will only diminish its potency. Nobody needs to know the details of what your intuition has to say, as its influence will express itself in your actions towards others.

3) *The more you ignore it, the less it will come out to express itself.* Never get frustrated with your intuition for not showing up on demand. Simply come back to the practices in this section, so it learns to trust you and has space to emerge.

Practices for Proper Energy Use

When we connect to Proper Energy Use, there is no such thing as HUS-TLE anymore! "Work" isn't about plowing through and making things happen, but about directing our already flowing energy through the attention cultivation and intuition practices above. We swap "working hard" for "aligning ourselves with the optimal outcome," thus entering the true flowstate and bringing our Elevated Capacity to life.

Any time you catch that "rat race" feeling in the body/mind—where self-created stress causes intense, obsessive thought patterns connected to chasing the competitive edge, staying on top, and completing your to-do lists—hit pause on your mental trajectory. This is your opportunity to REPURPOSE that intensity into cultivating Elevated Capacity—the merger of attention, intuition and proper energy use—by asking yourself the following questions in response to the "rat race" feelings:

1) *In what ways am I responding from a place of childhood programming and telling myself that working harder is the only way?*

2) *If I see or feel a roadblock in my path, instead of immediately pushing through it, can I first acknowledge the issue?* Can I acknowledge that "Okay yes, this is a problem, and I take full responsibility for it," and then ask: "How can I slow down and get more creative with my approach?"

3) *Before I develop an action plan, can I see a moment in the recent past when I neglected right action?* Examine a situation when you sacrificed your personal agency and explore how making a different choice might have prevented this self-created stress. Write out this chain of events and find the point of divergence.

As we explore and experiment with the concept of Elevated Capacity, we begin to dismantle our addiction to both Hustle and the idealized and elusive projection of Flow, which keep us trapped in the endless loop of over-production and "better time management" solutions while robbing us of our Intuitive Efficiency. By developing our Elevated Capacity instead, we learn to respect our rest and envision our work in the world as service to the collective. This is how we access new levels of creativity, with less self-created stress and more personal agency.

SUBTLE BODY PRACTICE
Potent Focus + Efficiency Mediation
This practice guides you towards Elevated Capacity; with single point-

ed focus, potency rises to the surface in this 30-day sadhana. As a result of this meditation's potent focus, it will help you befriend your Intuitive Efficiency—connecting with an inner voice that is expansive rather than prescriptive. This simple contemplative practice gives us access to listening with ease and responding without any self-created stress in the system. This creates key consciousness reference points within our meta-dialogue that help connect us to our Intuitive Efficiency and capacity for right action.

Posture

Sit in Sukhasana, or a simple, cross-legged seat. Prop yourself, if necessary, to support your body. Make this easy on your posture and feel free to lean against something. If knee pain is present, you can always straighten your legs and support your lower back, or sit in a chair.

Mudra

Palms facing the body, just in front of the heart space. Relax the elbows in the same plane for ease of posture. Place the palm of your right hand over the back of your left hand and bring the thumbs to touch. The hands are in front of the heart space (see image opposite).

Breath Pattern

This breath pattern is designed to create equal attention on intensity, stillness, and letting go. There is no mantra with this meditation, so the subtle attention is placed on the breath alone. In the absence of words, we learn to focus on more silent, embodied rewriting of patterns. When we commit to no longer avoiding stillness, we begin to see its medicinal qualities emerge.

Inhale for 5-10 seconds. At the top of the breath, hold for the same duration as the inhalation.

Then, a long slow stable exhale out of the nose, to the utter completion of the breath. Give it a moment to complete and allow the lungs to feel totally empty. Note where you are in the length of the breath pattern. As the length of the inhalation increases, the length of the inhalation retention can also increase.

Spine is still erect and mudra is still intact. Keep repeating this breath pattern for the duration of the practice with the eyes closed.

Timing
Practice 3 minutes daily for 30+ consecutive days.

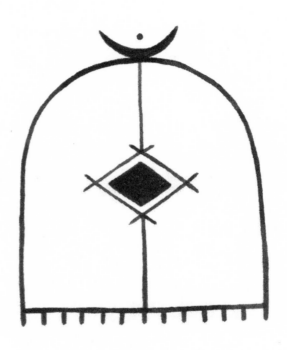

THE SIXTH BINARY
ROOT/CROWN: INTEGRATED BEING

Ann had worked intimately with me off and on, until she decided to dive into one of my deep study programs. About three months in, the same several issues kept arising in her path. I could sense on a deep level that these patterns had been repeating for decades. Naturally and perfectly, Ann had arrived with all of her subtle body imprints (a term I'll define later in the chapter)—playing on loop as if they were reality.

Childhood trauma, an alcoholic narcissistic mother, and a too-many-strings-attached relationship to her father formed the perfect storm of "Root" issues, which showed up in her dealings with money, sex, and power. Her lack of safety as a child, and volatile family unit as an adult, robbed her of the self-empowerment skills required to stand up for herself in the realm of sex and intimacy. An unhealthy obsession with spending, and an inability to see money objectively, was putting her own child's security at risk. And a constant, self-diminishing voice caused her to relinquish her power in professional and interpersonal relationships.

Her approach to dealing with this trauma was heady. A well-spoken and creative woman with a "seeker" Sagittarius stellium in her astrological chart, she hid the mess behind intellectual speech patterns, and obsessive purchasing of spiritual programs, sacred trinkets, and wellness products. Often, Ann would tell me about the meditation she was doing, and the years of spiritual study she had completed to date. On the extremely sensitive line between "meditating to disintegrate ego-structure" and "meditating to dis-associate," Ann had started to polarize towards the latter.

Regardless of how articulately she was able to intellectualize her own "issues" and "projected solutions," I wasn't seeing many "aha" moments in our work together. I realized that I had to cut through the intellectual circle-talking with bluntness, clarity, and intensity, risking her perception of the student/teacher relationship in order to help her create true transformation. In her daily actions, Ann was always asking for "more": more sadhana, more reading, more products, more course work. To which I said: NO MORE.

When we started to cut through the over-spiritualization, Ann and I began to understand how her Root energy, and her perception of Crown energy, were dramatically misaligned. This showed up in:

1) *Constant intellectualization of self and others.* There was always a complicated dramatic reason for her behavior, or interpretation of another person's behavior, in order to avoid personal responsibility around her lack of boundaries and self-respect in the realms of money, sex, and power.

2) *Bypassing her embodied truths and disempowering herself, while ignoring her emotions.* She had very little contact with or appreciation for her body, and was always bypassing its needs, demands, and important messages. Her body/mind was screaming for attention with many digestive and reproductive imbalances.

3) *Obsessions with "spiritual and creative" ideas that had no fertile ground to root down into.* By excusing away and not tangibly dealing with material issues like financial debt, Ann's creative desires and outward yearnings never had the grounding to manifest.

Whether it's working through physical and emotional abuse in their ancestral lines and previous partnerships, extreme fear around money, or debilitating self-worth issues, students consistently come to me with the desire to heal and confront a damaged Root. Many of these students have been practicing and meditating for years—over-intellectualizing their earthly issues with very little action. They tell me that they want to start their own business, manifest abundance, connect with their truth, and feel lighter and happier. But without integrating the Root end of the binary, they're lost in an endless loop that perpetuates past trauma and emotional immaturity—stalled in the movement between intellectualized spiritual practice and deep integration.

The Root/Crown binary arises anytime our earthly issues demand action and clarity, but we instead employ debilitating avoidance through layers of intellectualization, ignoring our embodiment and jumping into the Pollyanna clouds. Or, we polarize at the other end, chasing superficial fixes within the Root trinity of Money/Sex/Power, often believing that by securing certain expressions of these energies, we'll be "safe"—which keeps us stalled in a misaligned Root and unable to reach the inspired insights of the Crown.

The Root end of the binary connects us to the bottom three chakras (Root, Sacral, and Solar Plexus)—home to our earthly needs for basic safety, emotional regulation, and desire fulfillment. We all crave connection to this place, and yet often suffer from "Root Deprivation," which shows up in fear-based scarcity mentality. Capitalism itself is based on the exploitation of this Root Deprivation, as we're left constantly feeling that we need to consume more, and grasping from a place of never having, or being, "enough."

Root Deprivation can take many forms. At one end, we may view these "human" issues as somehow base, animalistic, or less evolved—seeking to deny and transcend these urges and move "higher." We may also believe that we should already have it "together" in these so-called basic areas, seeing them as simple fixes that don't really need to be investigated and are therefore bypassed. And at the other end, we may express our fear of lack by becoming obsessed with pursuing surface expressions of Money/Sex/Power—leaving us unable to access the Crown energies of compassion, objectivity, and clear communication.

And at the Crown end of the binary, we believe we can do no wrong— we believe we are realized, intuitive, enlightened, and infallible as the result of the spiritual power we've gained from psychic downloads, and manifestation practices that supposedly open our crown chakra and third eye. These shiny, "high vibe" parts of the binary capitalize on our tendency to avoid taking responsibility for our personal dramas, often connected to our Root. This is the shaky foundation on which commercial spirituality is often built, which promises success, happiness, and ease, but is based in extractive capitalism. Non-binary Crown energy, on the other hand, is not based in this quick-fix, bypassing model, but instead asks us to purely receive reality—without the distortion of the ego-structure, but also without the need to fully "transcend" the ego or disconnect from Root.

When we commit to breaking the Root/Crown binary, we open up to Integrated Being: a simple, clear state that allows us to do the work of being human without categorizing it as either "high" or "low," or more or less enlightened. Through this work, we fortify our capacity to truly receive. When we address Root Deprivation that causes us to get stuck in extractive cycles of "taking," we can be open to both sustainable earthly receiving and the pure, actionless receptivity of aligned Crown energy. In doing so, we develop an intuitive vision for how to "run" energy through our system—moving from constantly consuming all forms of energy to fill an insatiable Root Deprivation hole, and towards greater agency in choosing how to use our energy, which brings us ever-closer to both a solid Root and a receptive Crown.

THE MYTHS OF ROOT/CROWN

The Fake and Awake Myth
Her crown chakra is lit
I've found my teacher! (said after taking one, three-day online course with them)
With so many students, they must be legit—I'm in

"Spiritual success" is often equated with divine powers, psychic downloads, and awakenings that are all related to our upper energy centers and are thought to demonstrate a high level of spiritual prowess. The Root/Crown binary pushes many seekers to chase this sellable vision of "spiritual evolution," and to disassociate with our Root issues in order to pursue this dream of spiritual success. Even the phrase "We are spiritual beings living a human experience," used as commonplace vernacular nowadays, attempts to create hierarchy within our own self-understanding. We set off chasing the spiritual carrot while devaluing our lived human experience—even while many long-standing ancient teachings actually state that this human incarnation is not meant to be bypassed or seen intellectually as "less than."

Chasing this "Fake and Awake" way of life looks exactly as it sounds: we chase prescriptive end goals of happiness, peace, and fulfillment, while ignoring the real, moment-by-moment work that produces these states not as achievable aims but as byproducts of dealing with the intense, transformative work of looking at our Root issues. Packaged in phrases and concepts like "activation," "law of attraction," and "manifestation," this Fake and Awake Myth implies that we can somehow leap frog over the messy, uncomfortable work of being human to reach a static, elevated state of perfection.

We especially see this in our modern "guru" archetypes. Our vision of a "spiritually advanced" teacher often conjures an image of a being cloaked in white, covered in mala beads, and preaching about vegetarianism while countless students gather at their feet. This person is seen as "evolved," with an open crown chakra that can "stream truth." Many of us approach our gurus, life coaches, and self-help experts with an insatiable hole of Root Deprivation—coming to them to uncover a missing sense of purpose or to manifest "abundance." As a result, we often bypass these teachers' humanity and relationship to their own "Root," and the extreme effort and years of hardship that went into cultivating clarity within.

Whether through gurus and teachers, or programs promising quick-fix intuitive downloads, we often end up chasing an extractive version of Crown energy—seeking to get some of that authenticity for ourselves. But true Crown energy is about cultivating a pure state of receptivity, opening ourselves to be stripped of the meta-dialogue that creates obstacles so that we can dissolve and disintegrate Karma. In this model, there is "nothing" (pure consciousness) to gain and "everything" (egoic thoughts) to lose.

Trying to "get something" from these spiritual teachings and practices only reinforces our Root Deprivation, and blocks our ability to connect with the pure receptivity of an integrated Crown.

Before enlightenment, chop wood carry water; after enlightenment, chop wood carry water.

This brilliant Zen saying asks us to come down from the podium and re-member that spiritual growth, in its most realized form, is a never-ending process with legs out in the world. Why don't we hear about the Buddhist master who reached enlightenment and decided to remain a farmer, and would not accept gold for his teachings?

When we dress up our spiritual seeking with a shiny pink bow, we keep asking for "more" and chasing the next "high"—instead of choosing to resiliently engage with the daily, behind-the-scenes work of our lives on a moment-by-moment basis. When we view the movements of our lives here on Earth as the teachings themselves, we no longer need to label parts of human life as "less spiritual," and our work needs no pedestal. We realize that spiritual development can spring from inner simplicity that discerns rather than dissociates, and we open ourselves to having our misperceptions removed, rather than trying desperately to seek enlight-enment through engaging with yet more spiritual tools and teachings.

The Grounding Down Myth

You need more grounding in your life
You need to get back into your body
Walk on the earth barefoot and eat more root veggies to ground down

The over-use of "grounding" as a remedy for our culture's Root imbalanc-es has seeped into every single aspect of our wellness world. We place es-sential oils on the bottoms of our feet, post pictures of ourselves hugging trees on social media, and are fed marketing campaigns shot in pictur-esque nature surroundings.

And yet this fetishization of nature sidesteps the reality that much of our Root Deprivation is actually connected to the trauma done to the Earth by extractive capitalism—including both the over-extraction of resources and irreparable damage done to our "beloved sacred nature" by many of our daily modern lifestyle choices, and the displacement of many of our ancestors from their lands of origin and indigenous roots. Rather than digging deeper to consider what privileges and conveniences we might need to give up in order to repair our relationship to both planet Earth and our ancestry, we attempt to connect with Root Deprivation panaceas through surface "earthy" engagements that ultimately leave us with no real ground on which to stand.

While there is certainly something to be said for rebalancing the central nervous system by aligning our lives with the rhythms of nature, and for appreciating and preserving our planet's precious ecosystems, integration of the Root/Crown binary means encouraging less separation between us and our unique human needs. The "grounding" panaceas often end up creating more separation—both between those privileged enough to have access to untouched nature and organic, farm-to-table foods, and those who do not; and between us and our highly-individualized Root Deprivation profiles and needs.

Rather than adding to the situation with more grounding techniques or products, on a subtle body level we must understand why we feel groundless to begin with, and what interpersonal and intergenerational causes have created this feeling. It's also important to discern between groundlessness as an anxious state of mental confusion and bodily discomfort, caused by feeling untethered from our own existences; and the groundlessness that is actually a catalyst for growth—the feeling of partnering with all that is unknown and beyond our control.

Ask yourself what might be preventing you from realizing "groundlessness" as a valuable state of self-realization:

1) Is there emotional, verbal, or sexual abuse, in the past or from the family unit?
2) Is there an astrological emphasis on air or water in your natal

chart? These placements sometimes result in a headier intellectualization of our lives, or a strong emotional fluidity that sometimes tends towards the boundaryless.

3) What is causing depleted self-trust? Is it your own actions? Or staying in relationships and situations that diminish your self-worth?

4) Are your basic needs met adequately and predictably—meaning access to food, water, shelter, income?

5) Have you been relying on numbing agents to distance yourself from unmet Root needs?

6) Are your current relationships emotionally safe or unsafe? Do you have the space to express your full humanness in your relationships?

7) Do you have a community, family, or social network that is trustworthy and that you can count on?

Perhaps you get to the end of this inquiry and find, "I'm all air and water, have no regular income, and have no social network." If this is the case, imagine me greeting you with excitement, saying:

Groundlessness in and of itself is the point of attention for integration. Staying with these sensations, rather than immediately reaching to "get grounded," helps us get at the real drivers of our Root Deprivation without bypassing into Crown energy glorification.

Confronting the Grounding Down Myth helps us build on the work we've done to dismantle Fake and Awake Crown fetishization. When we let go of the commodified fairytale that walking barefoot through the woods is all we need to feel safe and supported, we instead cultivate a willingness to confront the real challenges of our own lives each and every day—seeing beyond high/low spiritual work to find the "ground" that springs from addressing the deeper holes of Root Deprivation that lie beneath the surface, and remaining completely available to stay with whatever work arises.

The Shadow Work Myth
In spiritual and wellness circles, the concept of "shadow work" seems to

be catching on like wildfire. This "work"—which supposedly rests on our ability to unearth and examine the less shiny places within us that many of us fear to tread—is positioned as part of our spiritual due diligence, and will lead to "spiritual success" as the result of our willingness to get messy.

Yet claiming that there is even such a thing as "shadow work" implies that there is "light work" on the other side. In this binary worldview thinking about shadow work, we actually see many binaries reinforced: light/dark, good/bad, high/low. Even when we claim that shadow work is necessary, it often functions as something that we must confront in order to transcend and transform—positioning the "shadow" as something dark, bad, and low, which must be elevated into something light, good, and high.

If we hold onto the idea that "light" is on the other side of shadow, this work becomes a form of both spiritual self-harm and narcissistic navel gazing that's less about making peace with and integrating our complexities, and more about "fixing" or moving "beyond" these parts. We become obsessed with digging out the shadow in order to gain something from the work—coming out the other side in some way improved. We see this in language like "If it's still coming up then you haven't resolved it"—the subtext being that we need to achieve completion and resolution of our shadow work, rather than grappling with and accepting the fact that personal and collective evolution is NOTHING BUT SHADOW WORK. In non-binary worldview, we are learning to integrate the deep spiritual realization that there is NOTHING waiting for us at the end of the tunnel: no reward, no finish line, no illusion of "betterment." Shadow work isn't something we choose to do when we feel like it. It IS THE WORK that we came into this world to do, in every moment.

In non-binary worldview, instead of "shadow work," we use the term "subtle body imprints," which refers to the complex network of lenses through which we view our ourselves and the world. When we categorize certain memories, events, actions, and personality traits as "bad," we often kick into victimhood rather than self-responsibility. Clarity, by contrast, is a state where NO BLAME is placed and full self-responsibility arises from all parties involved. Subtle body imprints are beyond category; they ARE the teaching this time around.

PERSONAL INQUIRY PRACTICE:
ROOT DEPRIVATION + CROWN ESCAPISM

This life of mine
Is the path
Step by step towards
Transformation
Liberation
Realization

My body as vehicle
My compassion as currency
My self-respect as the shield
My worth ethic as the tool
My clarity as the gaze
My ground of being, clear

Do not listen
To the seemingly polite
Lies of society
In the manifest form of
Money. Sex. Power.
Personal Power, the tipping point

Universal shifts, await.

Interrogating how the Root/Crown binary shows up for us means noticing where we are obsessed with an over-intellectualized version of spirituality that seeks enlightenment as "success." In tandem, it means looking at how we seek to fill our Root Deprivation hole from a more superficial outside force rather than our own organic, loving, and integral attention and self-respect.

Unpacking how this Root/Crown binary shows up in our lives means coming face-to-face with the concept of receptivity. Root Deprivation stems from a misaligned understanding of giving and receiving. When we don't have a clear handle on our Root Deprivation issues, we seek to "extract" resources—including "spiritual" Crown energy—to fill our perceived emptiness. The result is an emphasis on endless seeking and attainment, and an inability to give sincerely without subconscious strings attached. This, in turn, makes it very difficult to explore the action-less receptivity of our energetic power that is possible with an aligned Crown.

The Root Deprivation that we all carry is reinforced through our "trauma bonds"—those interpersonal and intergenerational relationships where self-worth is built on shaky ground. Through these bonds, we become addicted to repetitive actions that reinforce hierarchical definitions of value, success, and material security. But the stuff of our lives, as they are right now, is precisely where we can access stable, objective Root energy—the ground of our being. To access this stable energy, and move towards giving and receiving with greater awareness, begin by turning your attention to how the Money/Sex/Power Root Deprivation Trinity shows up for you.

The Money/Sex/Power Root Deprivation Trinity

While some schools of modern spirituality might deem the realms of Money/Sex/Power as "negative" or "corrupt," they only become detrimental when we don't consciously explore our relationship to them—when we act out of subconscious insecurity and overcompensating from perceived "lack" in these areas, instead of dealing with the nature of the deprivation that lies beneath. Reorganizing our Root Deprivation in each of these areas allows us to feel safe and secure so that we can repurpose our intellect to create less drama, worry, and anxiety, and free up the Crown to do what it does best: receive. When we do so, we are able to redefine our personal needs as they pertain to Money/Sex/Power, and can begin to repair our family units and communities through reciprocity rather than extractive attainment.

Start by exploring the realms of Money/Sex/Power in your own life:

Money + Root Deprivation

Within the Root/Crown binary, money is a relatively taboo topic—viewed as either the root of all "evil," or as a necessary resource that gives us greater freedom and power. Within non-binary worldview, by contrast, money contains a neutral charge and is often an extension of how we run prana and circulate energy. When we examine our unchecked Root Deprivation, we can envision money as simply part of a cyclical energy flow.

Free write all of your associations with money. Let it be a stream of consciousness to allow your psyche to make the big overarching connections. Reflect back upon this stream of consciousness to find a pattern, noticing your personal definitions, cages, and strings attached around money. These patterns are your projected frequency around money.

Sex + Root Deprivation

Within the Root/Crown binary, sex energy is limited to a body-specific desire and physical act. In non-binary worldview, sex energy moves beyond the physical to connect us to the initiatory spark of all creation. Root Deprivation arises when we reduce this energy to the physical act, craving sex acts to bring us back into our "bodies"—similar to the barefoot in the forest grounding myth—and expecting others to receive us when we haven't first cultivated the capacity to receive ourselves.

Free write about your usage and understanding of sex energy—making it a stream of consciousness to allow your psyche to make the big overarching connections. Reflect back upon this stream of consciousness to find a pattern, noticing your personal definitions, cages, and strings attached around sex. These patterns are your projected frequency around sex.

Power + Root Deprivation

Within the Root/Crown binary, power often becomes entangled with both money and sex, and with heteropatriarchal, hierarchical societal models where we either maintain power "over" others through domination, or "under" others through martyrdom and victimhood complexes. In non-binary worldview, we maintain awareness of our underlying motivations and are able to catch ourselves when we're tempted to seek "energetic returns" from the power positions we take. Root Deprivation arises in this realm when we find ourselves using others to bolster our own influence.

In this free-writing exercise please explore all of the places you feel Powerful and Powerless. Dig into the circumstances around each of these feelings, and notice any personal patterns that emerge within the embodied feelings of Powerful and Powerless. Tap into your personal and professional life to bring these lived moments into your conscious awareness.

Root/Crown Escapism Checklist

Alongside our investigation of Root Deprivation, we must also work to examine escapist versions of Crown energy that prevent us from dealing with our actual Root issues, making us unavailable to a purer form of Crown receptivity. Take an inventory of the Crown Escapism Archetypes listed below, noticing which might arise in your personality aspects, and pair this section with a review of the Fake and Awake and Shadow Work myths.

1) **The Intellectual:** Over intellectualizes EVERYTHING—emotions, easy decisions, relationship dynamics—and beats interpersonal situations to death by continually "discussing" them in their own mind or with others. Strokes the ego by being the smartest and most well-spoken in a situation. Lots of lip service and very little action.

2) **The Seeker:** Reads every book on the market, name drops, uses big spiritual words, and likes to cite all of the study programs and teachers they follow. Quotes lots of fancy "texts" with very little embodied experience or nuanced understanding, hiding avoidance of personal messiness within the well-adorned identity of being "on the path."

3) **The Commercial Mystic:** Looks the part with flowy clothes and tattoos of spiritual iconography. Art-directs picture-perfect "rituals" and uber spiritual gatherings for social media. Signs up for expensive manifestation courses, claims to be constantly "tapped in," and

frames each Root-deprived side-hustle as another "epic download."

4) **The Skeptic:** Always questions, in search of hard and fast "facts" that are rooted in the finite predictability of the material world. Needs over-simplifications and straightforward definitions. Has difficulty mobilizing creative energy, and trusting parts of themselves beyond logic. Ignores the emotional and spiritual layers of life, lacks the levity of playfulness, and is quite pessimistic in outlook.

You might find it quite embarrassing to identify with any of these archetypes out loud. But the more clearly we commit to seeing these tendencies within ourselves, the more we can both tend the Root Deprivation that lurks beneath and access a receptive Crown. In its most potent form, aligned Crown energy is completely action-less: we can't "do" Crown energy. And simply noticing where we attempt this helps us get closer to this action-less, purely receptive state.

And here we are, at the threshold of breaking the Root/Crown binary and priming the internal structure for receptivity. Hold on love; your life and your imprint on others and society is about to do a dramatic about-face into a space of service from a deep well of self-fulfillment. By stopping the grasping, and learning how to hold the frequency of receptivity in the realms of Money/Sex/Power, you are on the path towards becoming an Integrated Being.

BREAKING THE BINARY: INTEGRATED BEING

In the contemplative exercises above, we began to build a resilient container to examine Root Deprivation feelings, motivations, and behaviors—interrupting a spend cycle of swiping our pranic credit cards at the Root Deprivation vending machine. We also looked at where we might have been escaping into a misaligned Crown, relying on over-intellectualization and seeking "enlightenment" to fill our own unexamined Root Deprivation hole.

Now, we're ready to integrate. Integrated Being involves moving towards a sense of giving and receiving in earthly ways that are not borne from Root Deprivation. This in turn opens the pathway towards the pure, action-less receiving that is part of realized Crown energy. A realized Crown gives us the capacity to hear, feel, and sense the universal intel that is not created or stimulated through our own ego-structure, and thus to receive the inspiration, serenity, and truth that show us what we truly "need."

Simply put, Root/Crown integration happens as a byproduct of living with integrity, simplicity, and objectivity. Integrated Being is built on the following fluid principles:

1) Receive Situations in Their Entirety

I often make this joke when people ask me about meditation and how to quiet the mind:

"That's called death." Everyone laughs. Then I get a straight face and say: "No, seriously, quit trying to ignore the metamorphic movements of your life—the teaching is there, and not in learning how to bypass it while it sits right next to you with duct tape over its mouth." Commit to the belief that the "work" is always right here where you are, is never ending rather than goal driven, and is not predicated on any splits between less-evolved Root work and divinely-inspired Crown work.

Pre-meditation "Mind Watch":

Before you implement any sort of meditation technique—which many of us do too early in our practice because we are still addicted to goals and it helps us feel like we are doing something to achieve them—practice "receiving" by sitting in silence and engaging your attention in a MIND WATCH. Set it up as follows:

5 min watch
5 min write
5 min watch
5 min write

In the watching period, allow your mind to be an open reservoir: try *not* to watch your thoughts. In the writing period, try to recall all of the thoughts that arose without self-editing. Just dump it all out on the page. Practice this pre-meditation technique to prime the mind to be soft, agile, and aware.

2) Create a Closed Loop of Receptivity

You're exhausted, you listen anyway. You're feeling elated, you listen. You're feeling depressed, you listen. You are devastated with life events, or the behavior of another, you listen. You catch your tongue before you leap to respond and remind yourself there is no action in pure receptivity.

Once you develop this level of maturity in listening, you prime the system to be a closed loop of reciprocity. No validation is needed from outside sources. At first, you listen to the physical, earthly, real-time theater of life playing out in front of you. Over time, access to the full space/time continuum that is not tethered to the lived moment opens. There is nothing to "over-intellectualize" but there is a whole lot to witness! The combination of the Mind Watch and the Gates of Contemplation work (below) will sharpen the meta-attention.

3) Employ the Test of Simplicity and Clarity

If stories surrounding an action don't sound simple and clear, and feel caught up in a complex sea of shame and blame, you will know that they are based in Root Deprivation. Tread lightly in this space, and vow to examine how you attempted to receive with stipulation by not first fully receiving the layered truth of yourself and the totality of the situation.

As you decide what action to employ moving forward, ask:

Is this clear?
Is this simple?

When realization and pure receiving rise to the surface there is no drama; instead there is an inner understanding of, "aha, that's what occurred, and this is what needs to be done." The ego-structure is not always "excited" about these realizations because they are often beyond personal preference and the ego-structure itself. In the face of simplicity and clarity, Root deprived behaviors will often assert themselves very strongly. Practice holding space for these behaviors and their messages, while also continuing to push forward towards clarity and simplicity. With these three principles of Integrated Being intact, we're now ready to dive deep into the Gates of Contemplation so that we can begin to recognize this state of integration within.

The Three Gates of Contemplation

Realigning our relationship to Root/Crown energy asks us to run all people, places, things, opportunities, and ideas through the three "Gates of Contemplation": *Return, Reciprocity, and Self-Advocacy.* Attending to these gates creates powerful Root energy by allowing us to accept, give attention to, and transform subtle body imprints so that we can encounter all of ourselves without stipulation or self-degradation. Once this foundational function of our Root energy is respected and primed, pure receptivity in the form of Crown energy is possible, and we have access to receive the totality of others, ideas, ethereal downloads, and important universal intel.

Take these Gates of Contemplation out into the world. And when complex situations arise in the areas of Money/Sex/Power, practice "running" them through these gates. Simply sit with yourself to see how the Gates can provide clarity on how to change your behavior to simplify your life. I have listed multiple questions under each Gate to speak to the complexity of trauma, addiction, sexual abuse, maladaptive family units, societal trauma, and intergenerational trauma that must be addressed as we begin to access them. Tread with care, my love, take breaks, and give yourself unbridled compassion in this cleansing process.

Gate 1: Return. *What is the return—both physically and energetically?*
For each energy you give out, you experience a physical, energetic, and/or spiritual return. To integrate Root/Crown we need to be able to discern if the return is sought with integrity or if it comes with emotional attachment. This

can be tricky, because often our ego-structure rewards self-degrading returns with a dopamine hit. I often ask myself in as neutral a voice as possible, "What was the return?" Then I wait to hear if the answer is coming from a "new" more integral me, or an old me based on emotional attachments.

Ask Yourself:

Is this making me money in a self-respecting manner?

Is this creating emotional or spiritual fulfillment?

Is this creating safety and personal growth for me?

Or am I seeking Return from Root Deprivation?

Am I seeking a familiar return, even though it feels wrong in my gut?

Am I seeking hierarchical power in the situation, where power over others is the return?

Am I seeking my own safety by stealing the safety of others?

Gate 2: Reciprocity. *Is there energetic reciprocity here?*

After you have discerned the nature of the return, you peel back another layer of yourself and the person, place, or situation involved. Does this structure, person, or environment have the capacity to give back the same level of respect and room for growth that I am willing to give?

Ask Yourself:

Can this person, place, or situation give and receive in the same capacity as me?

Is it me that is holding back from sharing in reciprocity?

If I feel like this relationship is not reciprocal, can I sketch out how this dynamic emerged—tracking moments where I neglected my own self-respect or neglected to respect another?

Is this thing I agreed to a full soul body "yes"? Describe in detail what a full "no" and "yes" sound and feel like for you.

Or am I seeking Reciprocity from Root Deprivation?

Am I using my powers of manipulation and pretending I am being reciprocal?

Can I define and feel reciprocity in my heart? (Write out what this looks like for you.)

What past trauma or societal imprint am I holding on to that causes me to keep taking from others without learning to give/receive for myself?

Gate 3: Self-Advocacy. *Can I stand up for myself, my time, and my energy, no matter the perceived risk?*

If you do not receive return or reciprocity from the exchange, you graciously refrain from engaging in that situation any further. It is nobody's fault—it's clearly just not a mutually held container. Integrated Being in action looks like closing the container with as little violence as possible, by putting down the responsibilities that keep the interaction alive.

Ask Yourself:

Did I make myself a priority today, this week, this year?

Am I making life choices that leave energy and other resources in reserve to deal with unexpected issues that might arise?

Even if I am worried, scared, or unsure, can I be my own biggest support system anyway and show up for myself?

Or am I engaging with Self-Advocacy from Root Deprivation:

Am I hoarding my own energy, and always focused on myself?

Am I constantly trying to quench my own existential thirst to the detriment of others? Can I sit with my own feelings of deprivation instead of stuffing myself full?

Am I terrified to take personal responsibility, "using" others as my support system without acknowledging their needs, and seeking to "bond" with others through wounded behavior like gossiping or speaking poorly of others?

As you move through the spectrum of breaking the Root/Crown binary, you'll feel a deep sense of integration begin to rise to the surface of your meta-dialogue. In subtle yogic anatomy, the throat is the integration space for the Root and the Crown, where a new transcendent vernacular of self-expression can blossom. Integrated body language and behavioral sets enter your consciousness, creating cohesion, empowerment, and reciprocity.

SUBTLE BODY PRACTICE

The Tenses of Being Meditation

Often, when we discuss giving and receiving within the dichotomy of the Root/Crown binary, there is a picture-perfect vision of sitting knee-to-knee, eye gazing, and compassionately listening to one another with the sort of "good behavior" that constitutes non-violent safe space.

To break the Root/Crown binary status-quo, you must be willing to admit that you don't have it all "figured out," and drop any fancy Crown "performance" in favor of a simple, clear practice.

Posture

Sit in Sukhasana, or a simple, cross-legged seat. Prop yourself, if necessary, to support your body. Make this easy on your posture and feel free to lean against something. If knee pain is present, you can always straighten your legs and support your lower back, or sit in a chair.

Mudra

Gyan mudra with the thumb and Jupiter (index) finger touching on both hands. Keep all your attention in the arms, fingers, and mudra.

Mantra

Har Hare Hari (Hahd Ha-ray Ha-ree)
Wahe Guru (Wha-hay Goo-ruu)

The three syllables of Har are linked to the clearing of the Throat chakra—symbolizing integration in the heart and communication space—so that we can see our Root Deprivation with clarity and simplicity. The throat is also the bridge to deeply aware listening, which is the precursor to pure receptivity, and realized Crown energies.

As you chant *Har*, move the arms to flank the torso, hands down near hips, palms facing forward. Arms long, straight, relaxed.

As you chant *Hare*, bend the elbows to 90 degrees, the palm with mudra now faced down.

As you chant *Hari*, lift the forearms so that the mudra lifts as well, elbows hanging by sides and palms now facing forward.

Stay in this final mudra as you chant *Wahe Guru* in the same position as you chanted Hari. Then initiate the same mudra and mantra pattern again for the duration of meditation.

Timing
Practice at least 3 minutes daily (even better is 11-22 if possible!) for 30+ consecutive days.

III.
HIGHER
OCTAVES OF
CONSCIOUSNESS

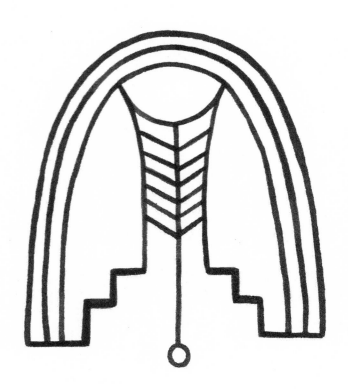

THE SEVENTH BINARY
ATTACHMENT/AVERSION: THE MIDDLE PATH

In Sasha's family unit, people pleasing ran in their blood. Exacerbated by expectations about the binary Feminine and its associations with self-denial, these habits in Sasha's family of origin felt inescapable to her. And with mostly air and water in her astrological chart, she had even more difficulty locating her own feelings and desires within the swirl of others' emotions.

The pressure to be in a relationship, "settle down," and start a family, was heavy. "It's just what you do," preached the social structure of her family, community, and educational environments. Before Sasha could identify what was happening, these limiting beliefs had seeped into her own subterranean landscape, and she had become deeply attached to a particular idea of safety, an insatiable need to be accepted, and the pursuit of things she didn't really want in exchange for social praise.

Her fierce Attachment to being in a relationship at all costs hid a deep Aversion to self-advocacy. This kept her stuck pining for an abusive ex-partner. Let's zoom in and feel the complexity of Sasha's Attachment/Aversion binary personified through her story:

Walking down the street she and her family always used to walk down together on Sunday morning, Sasha catches a frightening thought and her body cowers in the oversized jacked she hides within.

It was one of those moments when you are so disappointed with yourself, but somewhat grateful at the same time, that you can hear the subconscious reality rising to the surface:

I miss him, and his wool mittens, holding my small always gloveless hands. We must have appeared carefree to the onlooker—our arms swinging in cadence with both of our strides.

A brief moment of self-disgust arises simultaneously in the sunny crisp air as she reminds herself of his emotional and physical abuse. The many times she felt so tiny and disconnected, looking in the mirror, picking clothes that would cover her bruises and wounds.

The many times she felt like a hollow shell standing over the stove making his dinner. Resenting his laugh, knowing that on a truthful level she didn't have access to expressing spontaneous joy, because of the emotional cage he kept her in.

Her eyes start to water. But she won't call it "crying over him" anymore. He doesn't deserve that emotion from her.

Sasha feels so conflicted in the liminal space of missing his familiarity, but not the abuse. Deep down, she is disappointed with herself for not honoring the strength it took to run away and start over. She wonders: will this pattern ever just fucking STOP? On a cellular level it makes her sick to know she might, just maybe, have heard herself grieve for the loss of her abuser.

Although extreme, Sasha's pattern of "craving the familiarity of something we know is harming us" arises for all of us in some area of our lives. We attach to the comfort and safety of what we know, even when this perpetuates painful behavioral loops. When we consider the true impact of keeping the person, place, behavior, or version of self we have become bound to in our life, it doesn't seem "logical." And yet Attachment to patterns rooted in what we think we want and desire, and Aversion to things we don't want to face, seem to run on autopilot.

In classical eastern realms of thought, human suffering is said to arise because of our personal Attachment to ever-changing phenomena. Intellectually, this seems to make sense. Change is inevitable. Therefore, in simple lay terms: "I suffer because I am attached to things whose nature it is to change." Where we get tripped up is that we believe change itself causes suffering; when in fact it is our unwillingness or inability to keep pace with this change by adapting our ideas and beliefs about self, others, and the nature of reality. The more we cling to certain notions about the "way things are" and the "way we are," the more we get caught in a deadlock of confusion and cognitive dissonance.

Underneath this inflexible "conditioning" is a complex network of preferences—likes and dislikes—that forms the bedrock of the Attachment/Aversion binary. We cling to these likes and dislikes, and call this "who we are." Yet the more we cling, the more we deny the inevitable flux of life, and therefore the fluid identity that is needed for us to respond to the shifting reality of our lives. Paradoxically, when we look closely, we notice that we're actually also "attached" to our Aversions—forming a sense of self that's built on both what we perceive we "like" or "are," and what we say we "dislike" and are "not."

As we become increasingly attached to these preferences, they often get hidden within us—subconsciously motivating our behavior and leading to a lack of self-honesty that affects our relationships with others. Unexamined ideas about both what we're clinging to, and what we're pushing away, lead to implicit bias when relating to others, and result in entrenched relationship dynamics. We become addicted to self-recognition based on past programming that feeds our preferences—seeking to "see" and "find" a stuck version of our self in our relationship with others and the world, and unable to truly see the full evolutionary possibilities of both our self and the person or people who stand before us.

I once had a student ask me this brilliant question:

How do I deal with the complexity of attachment if I know the impulse or idea I am seeking over and over again feels good on one level, but is destroying my life on another?

As in Sasha's story, whenever we deem something "good" or "bad," we create energetic stagnation around that person, place, thing, or idea. As a result, we cling to a part of the "self" that identifies with that Attachment

179

or Aversion, and is therefore unwilling to change. When we try to break Attachment to "bad" habits that feel "good" on some level, we often adopt a binary stance. We hear this in statements like: *I am getting rid of things that no longer serve me.* Yet examining why this can sometimes be so difficult (if something is "no longer serving" then surely it should be easy to let go) provides very important intel into the roots of our preference structure: what ideas we're clinging to, and what we're disavowing.

Imagine this situation: You quit smoking, using all of your willpower. And then you find yourself at a crosswalk, waiting for the light to change. The person next to you is smoking and you take a few deep inhalations because you miss it and you still love the smell. But of course, there's no way you would actually smoke a cigarette. This is the complex territory that exists beyond the Attachment/Aversion binary and its connotations with good/bad.

In any given moment, each one of us is an amalgamation of alternate states of perception and comprehension. To feel this complexity is to acknowledge the impermanent state of our own humanity. Breaking the Attachment/Aversion binary and walking the "Middle Path" is about inquiring into this complex merger of motivation, action, and outcome.

We can start to do this by asking *who is attached to what*, and therefore *who is observing what we so quickly label as good and bad.* Keep in mind that your answer to this will most likely reveal several layers of identity to explore.

Who is acting? Who is expecting? Who is seeking validation? What is their motivation?

When we begin to ask "who" in many different forms, we see the "self" as a series of causes and conditions, not necessarily a rock-solid identity that needs things to be a certain way and is resistant to change. The inquiries in this chapter will be gut-wrenchingly real. Notice your own strong Attachments and Aversions to my words. Each time you feel a strong sensation, know that BINGO, you are needling the subterranean belief system that defines your ego-structure.

The end goal of this work is not to strip you of your human preference—nor is this even a possibility. Instead, breaking the Attachment/

Aversion binary means releasing our obsession with seeking control and stability through the illusion of an unchanging self and Universe. In doing so, we create a more agile, contemplative consciousness, with more capacity to hold compassion for the many points of view that lie beyond our personal likes and dislikes.

THE MYTHS OF ATTACHMENT/AVERSION

The Love Versus Fear Myth

Everything is motivated by either LOVE or FEAR
If you're not choosing love then you're choosing fear. Which do you want?

In binary worldview, we become "attached" to love and averse to "fear," and the belief that we are faced with choosing either one or the other is the foundation of much modern self-help rhetoric. Yet the causes and conditions that constitute any given situation contain seeds of both loving Attachment and fearful Aversion. In creating opposition between them, we become unable to see how they are connected. The more we push fear away, the more it hides within our expression of so-called love, and we end up "loving" out of fear. Imagine if, instead of reassuring those closest to us with the words "I love you," we instead inquired deeply of them: *What are you afraid of?*

When was the last time you asked yourself:

If my partner died, how would I respond?
What would I do without them?
Would I still recognize myself?
Am I the same with them and without them?

Instead of confronting and welcoming fear (of separation, of difference, of conflict) within our relationships, we often attach to ideas about a binary, all-consuming "love" that bypasses the teachings of fear. In an attempt to protect both our own Attachment to this limited expression of love, and our Aversion to the changing parts of ourselves and others, we forgo the whole truth of our relationships and cling to forms of "loving" behavior that are actually built on a half-truth. Our love becomes based on stipulation: only given if the other person validates the form of our self we are most attached to.

I love you because ...
I love you when ...
We are family, of course I love you ...

I see these kinds of conditioned-based engagements with love in my students' relationships all the time:

In the choice of a partner on whom to scapegoat personal issues; in an attachment to being "the evolved one" or always being "right" while attributing "wrongness" to other people and factors outside of ourselves; in perpetually "looking for love," but having a long list of lofty requirements that actually stagnate self-growth.

And outside of romantic relationship, we can see this in spiritual approaches that preach "love and compassion," yet base their principles on an elevated code of conduct that claims to be more "evolved" or "awake" then others—weaponizing the love/fear binary to claim that love is the higher, more desirable state we must reach by transcending fear, while perpetuating fearful interactions. How many times have you felt nervous to say something out loud—because you were afraid the other person wouldn't be able to accept it, but also because if you declared it you would in fact have to change?

When we commit to breaking our Attachment to one form of love, and our Aversion to fear, we discover an unconditional love that transcends right/wrong and good/bad by not placing blame. Self-awareness and clear communication become possible. Breaking our identification with the Attachment/Aversion binary shows us that true LOVE has no opposite.

The Mirroring Myth

When we are triggered by another person, we often say to ourselves:

Oh, they are displaying something I haven't healed in myself yet and it's getting mirrored back to me

Our need to create a story around pain, discomfort, trauma responses, and destructive emotions is only human; we make meaning through myth, story, and imagination in order to create a continuity of self. Yet, when we get caught in the Attachment/Aversion binary, the idea of "mirroring" can make us more susceptible to taking on another person's or a societal system's version of reality, without fully examining our own.

When we look at this through the lens of the Attachment/Aversion binary, we realize that the uneasiness and intense emotion that arise when we're triggered by another person is actually not a mirror. Instead, it's a clear indicator of our personal contribution to the situation, which tells us where, and how, we are attached to a certain part of our own self-image, and are averse to other areas of our body/mind where we fear to tread. We're "triggered" precisely because the situation is asking us to look at these Attachments and Aversions, and to adapt—choosing different behaviors and a revised understanding of our identity.

Consider the following example:

Kate and Hollie are business partners and long-time friends with a sisterhood quality to their relationship. Hollie finds herself constantly frustrated by her perception of Kate's behavior within their relationship, thinking:

"Kate is so disrespectful in her actions, she always drops the ball and doesn't acknowledge the work I have done on her behalf all of these years. If I want this project to survive, I will have to step in and fix her mistakes."

Kate and Hollie have experienced many arguments around this power dynamic. It is becoming increasingly frustrating to Hollie, while Kate continues the same behavior and frankly can't see any fault in her actions.

At this point, if Hollie used the Mirroring Myth to understand their relationship dynamic, she would stop at a mere reflection—making Kate's work *her* work, by believing that what she dislikes in Kate is something she needs to heal in herself. She might ask herself where she drops the ball in her own life, or conclude that she needs to practice letting things fall apart in the wake of Kate's actions. But when Hollie commits to examining the complexity of the situation more clearly, she's able to ask larger, more personally-responsible questions:

How and why am I allowing this sort of behavior from Kate over and over again?

What parts of me are being validated by saving her and this project from failure?

Why am I not willing to let go of this validation? If I let it go, what will be the consequence?

If I stop "saving her and the project," what will I really lose?

As Hollie digs deeper, she uncovers that if she stopped "saving" Kate and the project, she would lose Kate's admiration for her as the "strong savior type," and may in fact lose the entire relationship because it's built on these egoic "Attachment hits:"

1) Kate plays it small and takes zero responsibility for her life, which gives her the egoic hit of never dealing with the pain of failure.

2) Hollie likes being the capable, strong savior, and she will lose that emotional reinforcement from Kate if she makes the choice to no longer save her.

The truth is that no two humans hold the same subtle body imprints, karmic lessons, or dharmic purpose. When you find yourself triggered, ask:

To which parts of this relationship am I attached, and which aspects of my personal-

ity are receiving validation from this?

To which parts of this am I feeling deep aversion, and which aspects of my personality
are receiving validation from this?

Everyone projects; it's inherently human to seek to validate our own existence
(often at the expense of another person's uniqueness). But when we examine
how we seek these hits of validation, we start to move beyond an ego-structure that's built on Attachment/Aversion, and towards the Middle Path.

The Opposites Myth
True vs False
Good vs Bad
Right vs Wrong

When we set these states up as opposites, binary worldview means we
end up "grasping" or "clinging" to each end with equal intensity. In some
ways, this can be said of all the binaries: whichever end we give more focus to creates in us a growing inability to reckon with the other. In the
Attachment/Aversion binary, we have the chance to confront this head
on because this binary is the most fundamentally connected to the pain/
pleasure binary, which is what births so many of the "likes and dislikes"
that fuel our complex states of misperception.

This is the myth that's hiding in plain sight. But I couldn't just say
this out of the gate. Many of us can't grasp that we are actually attached to
our own aversions, and often, as a result, attached to the self-hatred and
shame that's sparked by pushing parts of ourselves and our experiences away. Each time we move "towards" or value the pleasurable/good/
like end of any binary, we unwittingly hide from what lies at the other
end—repressing our aversions even further and adding to their shameful
"charge." When a student in session says to me: *I am embarrassed to say the*
real thought out loud, I know we are getting somewhere truthful.

Because it's so hard for the intellect to understand that, to an extent, we "like" our "weird shit," we often seek to hide and protect our Attachment to our Aversions. Now, instead of examining and releasing this hidden Attachment, we end up clinging harder to the experience of shame, guilt, and self-hatred. But when we are willing to explore the chemical reactions of shame, guilt, and self-hatred—and the Aversions they are protecting—head-on, we often discover Attachment to buried belief systems that are unconsciously motivating our behavior.

Consider the following:

When we start working together, Callie boldly tells me that she wants to dismantle the patriarchy. We dig deeper, and then she says: "I want to disrupt the male gaze." We do more targeted subconscious work together, and she tells me: "I think the male gaze has even infiltrated the female gaze ..."

When we finally get to the root of it, she realizes that by pointing the finger at the patriarchy, she has neglected to tell herself the truth about what is motivating her own actions. Having been divorced for years, she says to me: "I realize I still do things to impress my ex-husband, as if he were watching."

Her Aversion to patriarchy and the male gaze is, in part, the way she frames her unwelcome Attachment to judgment from her ex-husband—she remains attached to his emotional abuse, and this motivates self-sabotaging actions in her present life. By looking at this Attachment to a self-hating pattern with her ex, she sees that what she is most averse to on the surface—the patriarchy—is fueled by a deeper Attachment to this pattern of being judged by him. And that pushing this down and remaining averse to dealing with it actually results in a kind of obsession with it that fuels so much of her behavior without her conscious awareness.

Now that we are starting to see the multi-layered identities that get built upon the Attachment/Aversion binary, let's dive into the personal complexities that pave the way towards the Middle Path.

PERSONAL INQUIRY PRACTICE:
IDENTIFY YOUR ATTACHMENT/AVERSION "HITS"

I see the divine demons
Of Fear, Shame, Self-Hatred & Guilt
Obscuring my divine complexity
Bear witness to facets of my inner world
Attention is the medicine
Transmutation is in the action

The Full truth, not just portions of it.
Can I tread alone,
In the dark waters of my psyche?
Can I stand in my steadfastness
To realize parts of myself I too push away?

I vow to no longer dismiss myself
Or reduce another
In my search for Love.
Skillful Means, Radical Self-honesty
Unshackling myself
From subconscious persuasion

I walk The Middle Path
With a willingness to hold my own paradox.
I am the cohesive
Loving
Space Between.

The Attachment/Aversion binary keeps us from considering our own complexity and the complexity of others, the true motivations for our behaviors, and the flux in our identities and our lives. To move beyond this mode of operating and with the inevitable flux of change, we need to first look at where we seek emotional Attachment/Aversion "hits" that affirm our "fixed" sense of self-identity.

For the inquiry below, pick a complex situation, relationship pattern, family dynamic, or mindset hang-up that seems to be playing on repeat in your waking life. I love to tell my students to pick a situation that will create the most "bang for their spiritual buck." Ideally, this situation contains questions that linger from previous sections of this book. Because the Attachment/Aversion binary fuels our "default" behavioral mode, it can often hide buried within other binaries.

As you review this situation, start by simply asking yourself:

What emotional "hit" do I keep seeking when I engage in this repetitive behavior?
What am I seeking to affirm about myself, another person, or the world at large, by continuing to behave in this way?
What beliefs am I attempting to protect?

Now take your inquiry further using the questions below, keeping in mind that, depending on the situation, Attachment and Aversion can moonlight as one another. Test your ability to see beyond the binary by reflecting upon complex situations that are full of emotion, triggers, and intense relationship dynamics. Explore how the "charge" of a given situation contains a mixture of both Attachment and Aversion.

1) *Where am I attached to how others see me, or how I see myself, in this situation?* Clearly explain some of the motivations for any egoic validation you're seeking.

2) *What self-identity aspect might I be attached to in this situation?* You might give it a nickname, like being the "perfect" one, the "victim," or the "savior."

3) *Am I attached to an outcome that feels forced?* Examine your unwillingness to pivot or to take more responsibility for a situation. What are you protecting in this unwillingness?

4) *Where am I attached to safety and reliability in this situation, perhaps at*

the expense of growth? What am I afraid to sacrifice if I choose to let myself, others, and the situation, grow and evolve?

5) *Am I attached to an emotional state because that's all I have ever practiced?* List these habitual modes of reacting, exploring why you play out behavior that is self-sabotaging yet familiar. There is no "right" answer here, just the intel of the reflection process.

6) *What do I often say I "hate"?* What drives me nuts about other people? What types of behavior am I often quick to judge or dismiss? And when and where in my life do I tolerate these things I "hate" and why? How might I seek to cover up those behaviors or qualities in myself? Be honest with yourself: do you actually engage in some of these behaviors or exhibit these qualities when no one is watching?

7) *What do I feel extreme aversion to within larger cultural and political systems?* How might I actually be contributing to this in my personal life or community?

8) *What people/places/things/systems do I complain about often?* Can I hear myself when I am complaining—do I actually enjoy this state of being? Listen carefully.

9) *How has past programming, religion, upbringing, and education conditioned me to validate myself and others through the good/bad binary?* Write out an example of a moment in your life when you needed to do something right by yourself, but others judged your actions as inappropriate. What was it like to hold this paradox in your inner body?

10) *What simple inner behavior drives me nuts, but am I embarrassed to say aloud?* We often protect our attachments to self-destructive behavior with a barricade of feelings: embarrassment, shame, guilt, victimhood. By staying with these feelings, we can use these chemical sensations as messengers to help us uncover where we are clinging.

Take a full 30 days to allow this inquiry to take shape. These inquiries are deep; once you think you have hit the bottom, I promise you there will be a trapdoor in your ego-structure. Keep going there, again and again. Give yourself the necessary time and space, and be deliberate about this.

Not all of these questions will deeply resonate, and that's perfectly alright. Pick the 3-5 that carry the most "charge" and record your evolving answers—looking for a clear, repeating pattern that reveals some of the strongly-held self-identity beliefs that keep you bound to your own form of the Attachment/Aversion binary. Lastly, take a look at your "motive": the reason you've employed this behavior in order to protect something within yourself that you've been unwilling to evolve.

Within all of this inquiry, keep these three central questions in mind:

What personality aspects am I deeply attached to?

In what ways do I hide my Aversions from myself, and in doing so reinforce my own Attachment to them?

What is the larger motive behind clinging to these Attachments and Aversions? What parts of my self-identity do I go to great lengths to protect, even if it means continuing behavior that prevents change and personal evolution?

List out these emotions, thought-patterns, and versions of self clearly for each situation.

If we define our self-identity by: *I AM this* and *I AM NOT that*, then to cultivate equal-minded Middle Path awareness we must contemplate both statements with equal value. Uncovering both what we think we ARE and ARE NOT helps us begin to see that we are in fact so much more than our Attachments and Aversions to these ways of being—freeing us up to evolve our self-identity, our relationships, and our response to life. Over time, we remember that we are actually the cohesive, loving space that exists between.

BREAKING THE BINARY: WALKING THE MIDDLE PATH

While teaching a workshop entitled "Confronting Destructive Emotions: The Dirty Work of Happiness," I encountered a 50-something-year-old woman who kept playing with her rose quartz mala beads during the three-hour session. As the session unfolded, she appeared to be bored and distracted, so when she raised her hand to pose her question, I was excited by her engagement.

A question in open public drop-in workshops is almost always accompanied by a long, complex storytelling moment to front load the inquiry. As a teacher I listen more deeply to this than I do the question itself, and this woman's story revolved around the turmoil of her marriage and the emotional abuse being perpetuated on both sides. In her speech, there was a yearning to be seen as a "good yogi" and to affirm she was not attached to the outcomes of their arguments, even though her tone and body language was telling us a completely different story.

In the middle of this story, she abruptly asked me:

So I should practice non-attachment, and let him do what he wants and work it out himself? Divorce is not an option. I will do anything else in the world but that.

The subtext of her question was clear:

How can I live with what I abhor when I am unwilling to leave?

I responded with a story that debunks the commonly-held belief that non-attachment means neutrality, inaction, and passivity. I spoke of China's Communist regime and its invasion of peaceful Buddhist territory, explaining that amidst the slaughter of the Tibetan people, monks did not just sit passively, practicing "non-attachment" on their meditation cushions. They took extreme action through skillful means that matched the intensity of their oppressor, lighting their robes on fire in public squares as protest—saying: "You can kill me and my people, but you can never take my dignity and freedom."

In binary worldview, the concept of non-attachment is often used to describe not attaching to outcomes, but this understanding of it perpetuates passivity and a lack of Spiritual Agency. In non-binary worldview, by contrast, walking the Middle Path means practicing "healthy attachment," which does not mean tolerating things that contain deep pain or violence and calling it neutrality, "yoga," or rising above. Instead, it means actualizing your desire in a way that's clean, respectful, and in integrity. It's not that we're trying to purge all of our strong responses and become totally detached; but that we're committed to witnessing our Attachments and Aversions in action, and the motivations that lie beneath, and releasing from our clinging to preference so we can adapt to life and evolve our identities and responses.

Within this fluid field of witnessing and adapting, we can develop a sense of humor about what we cling to, which leads us to the true definition of humility. We come to know our perfectly-timed, programmed responses that arise from past preferences like the back of our hand. And in doing so, we can catch them before we seed them in the present moment through unconsciously motivated behavior. Middle Path action springs from no longer attaching to the past Attachment/Aversion binary structures we used to cling to.

Follow the steps below for a "Mindfulness Technology Upgrade" that will help rewire any binary worldview Attachment/Aversion programming and move you closer to the Middle Path.

Step 1: Drop Your Attachment to "Intention"

When we say, "Well that wasn't my intention," we often engage in bypassing the intensity, pain, and suffering of both self and other. Our intention doesn't affect how another person perceives a situation and is not a valid vehicle for keeping up with the rate of change. Shifting the frequency of a relationship, a professional setting, or a social structure happens in the action space—not in the well-wishes of intentions.

When you commit to witnessing your own urge to act from the Attachment/Aversion binary, and instead respond with less preference and expectation, you are able to become more aware of the effects of your actions, and the objective witness of another person and their reactions. When we drop the blame, judgment, and explanation-seeking of "intention," everyone involved has greater access to choosing behavior that is morally dynamic.

Step 2: Get Clear About Your Motivations

As we began to explore in the Personal Inquiry Practice, when we examine our Attachments and Aversions and look at the beliefs that lie beneath, we can start to see the full truth. We are inherently wired to self-preserve, and to seek to see our identity and ego-structure reflected out in the world. It is impossible to remove all "agenda" from our actions. Walking the Middle Path simply means that every time we reach outside of our own energetic container, we commit to developing our awareness, and learning something about our own internal structure that is built on conditioned preference.

Remember: THERE IS ZERO PASSIVITY OR NEUTRALITY in the practice of healthy attachment. There is only an extreme willingness to check our motivations; and when we are clear that the motive behind our attachment is not one rooted in the confusion of the good/bad, fear/love, pain/pleasure binary, we know it is healthy attachment, and that the outcome of our efforts is something worth pursuing.

Let's take a simple example:

"I want to run my own business and work for myself."

We might probe our deeper motivations and discover an addiction to society's praise for being successfully self-employed. Or a desire to escape the 9-to-5 grind and "have more time to ourselves." On top of that, we might be attached to a fantasy version of what entrepreneurial life looks like, and be allowing these fantasies to dictate our future projections of outcome.

None of these desires are "wrong"; we are naturally always in a state of creation and action as humans. Healthy attachment happens when we acknowledge our Attachment to these end goals, while also looking beyond these egoic fantasies of future accomplishment. We begin to become less concerned with future projections, fears, and even public opinions and responses, and this frees up energy to actually find joy in the process. For instance, if the entrepreneur in the above example softens around the desire to "have more time for themselves," releasing the hard and fast grasping to this principle as an end goal, this "time" starts to naturally occur.

Step 3: Cultivate Skillful Means

I am not attached to the outcome …

Guess what? Yes, you are! ALWAYS.

We are all human. We all have desires and unconscious belief systems that motivate our actions. We need to be attached to an outcome to some degree, or else we wouldn't put forth the intense energy, and powerful, hardworking effort to accomplish anything. Our attachment to outcomes is why it can be so difficult to watch something die or to put down a project.

The difference between binary Attachment/Aversion, and the healthy attachment of the Middle Path lies in the level of *skill* in our attachment to outcome and recognition of motive. This means being clear on our motive so that we can wholeheartedly pursue a desire, relationship, or endeavor by focusing on the transformative process itself, rather than fixed end goals or demands upon others.

Bring to mind a situation where you can feel your Attachment to outcomes firing. Developing skillful means involves remembering that:

Desire is normal and human
It's okay to desire to "do" and "have" many things in this incarnation
If I suppress all Attachments, I will cling to my Aversions
I must clearly examine my motives, for they are the stickiest part of this process
I must ask: have I considered the state of being this desire will require of me? Of others?

Step 4: Be Ready to Leave Something Behind

When our only motivation in a situation is one of preserving old versions of self out of habit, we cannot identify healthy attachment and access skillful means.

To recap: *Healthy attachment is a desire to change at the rate that our consciousness is expanding.*

Ask yourself: *Is my identity evolving at the same rate as the situation I am perceiving?*

This is the pinnacle question of walking the Middle Path!

Committing to our evolution and personal transformation over any externally-fixed measures of validation means there will be some necessary "loss" involved. Often, I ask myself: what will I lose if I dive in head-first to pursue this desire? Can I live with that? Can I imagine a daily life flow with that loss? What impact will that loss have on my identity?

By asking these penetrating questions, we also address our cultural Aversion to loss itself, and acknowledge its valuable role in breaking the Attachment/Aversion binary. When we unknowingly cling to anything out of a fear of loss, it actually leaves no room for us to pursue new things from a place of healthy attachment; and we wind up trapped in a binaried identity, "hoarding" old Attachments that no longer reflect our personal evolution. Walking the Middle Path means walking the path of the phoenix day-in and day-out: loosening our grip on out-dated Attachments as we evolve beyond them, and facing our Aversion to ego-death in the name of being continually reborn.

SUBTLE BODY PRACTICE

Meditation to Balance Meta-Dialogue, Motive, and Projection

This is one of the meditations that I use most often in my personal practice, because of its profound ability to pull the complexity of our ego-structure to the surface, in turn helping us project less and reveal more of our authenticity. It was gifted to me by one of my teachers, as are several of these practices.

This practice helps us cultivate our ability to see, feel, and respond to Middle Path awareness by aligning our meta-dialogue with our motive and projection. Oftentimes, the energetic feeling of being "inauthentic" springs from leaving our Attachments and Aversions unexamined, and therefore creating an identity that's built on subconscious motivations and outward projections. The subtle work of this meditation helps bring this latent internal conflict to the surface of your awareness.

Posture

Sit in Sukhasana, or a simple, cross-legged seat. Prop yourself, if necessary, to support your body. Make this easy on your posture and feel free to lean against something. If knee pain is present, you can always straighten your legs and support your lower back, or sit in a chair.

Mantra

Sanskrit: स त न म

Sa: Birth
Ta: Life
Na: Death
Ma: Rebirth

Chant this mantra at a rhythm that suits you as an internal vibration. Chant the mantra in your mind—no need to chant it out loud. This creates more subtlety in the relationship to your own sound current.

Mudra

Relax the elbows down near the sides of the body with little effort. Open the fingers, with the palms open and face up. Touch the edges of the Sun (ring) fingers on both finger pads, and naturally the Mercury (pinky) fingers will gently cross. Keep the left Mercury finger above the right in the mudra.

Mudra Action with Mantra

Begin to chant *Sa Ta Na Ma*, rhythmically and silently in your mind, without rushing.

Match each syllable with the following mental mudra:

Sa: Tense the tip of both Jupiter (index) fingers and the thumbs
Ta: Tense the tip of both Saturn (middle) fingers and the thumbs
Na: Slight pressure between the touching Sun (ring) fingers
Ma: Tense the pad of the thumb and the tips of both Mercury (pinky) fingers.

Set the timer for 11 minutes, stay still, and focus on your easy seat. Use the mental mudra and mantra to keep the meta-attention engaged. Recite the mantra with clarity and a willingness to balance the meta-dialogue, motive, and projection.

Timing

Practice 11 minutes daily for 30+ consecutive days.

THE EIGHTH BINARY
SELF-WILL/DESTINY: KARMA + DHARMA

People often approach the question of Self-Will/Destiny with an all-or-nothing mentality. At the Destiny end of the binary, we hear language like:

I will leave it up to fate
It's written in the stars—it's our destiny
It's in God's hands now; I trust the higher plan

The divine (no matter the personal language we use to describe it) is certainly looking to collaborate with us on a millisecond by millisecond basis. But when we polarize into binary Destiny, we engage in what almost becomes a form of internal gaslighting—denying the existence of our own Spiritual Agency and the personal will that's available for us to exercise inside the limits of a given situation.

On the other end of the spectrum is the diehard individualism of the Self-Will obsessed:

You can do it: work hard to create the life you want
Everything is a choice, and you have the power
Put your mind to it and all is possible

Recognizing where you're stuck in victimhood mentality and building trust in your own capacity to help yourself is an extremely valuable part of developing radical self-awareness. But binaried Self-Will leaves very little room to increase our personal sensitivity to nuanced contexts and to the entire energetic system—so we can see the distinction between what we can and cannot control. Operating solely from the Self-Will end of the binary can lead to intense burnout, feelings of personal failure, and a constant misaligned hustle that prevents flowstate and universal collaboration.

Both ends of this binary result in some level of exhaustion on the spiritual path, as we either try to Self-Will ourselves into a socially constructed box of "success," or hide in the passivity of a Destiny that relinquishes all Spiritual Agency to a divine order outside of the self.

Let's look at a few behavioral sets that manifest within the Self-Will/Destiny binary:

The Self-Created Stresser: Someone who is always "pushing the river" and fighting against the larger forces in life. Constantly exclaims how busy and full life is, and sweats *everything*. Wears suffering as a badge of honor, claiming that breakthroughs and moments of triumph are sweeter because they represent the challenges that got them there. The Self-Created Stresser claims that they have the personal power to get through any hardship—operating from the mentality that the juice is only worth the squeeze if you have to suffer, and failing to see that the difficulty they're enduring is often self-created. Destiny is "fought for" through the application of misaligned Self-Will.

The Perpetually Fatigued: At the other end of the binary, we find someone who is totally helpless, with stunted Self-Will. Lacks passion and the human grit required to take full responsibility for their own shortcomings and internal struggles. Not all these actions are "conscious"— oftentimes, they'll endure long periods in which they lack the time or capital to invest in self-care. These periods of time are the result of a protection mechanism they unconsciously perpetuate from past hardship, which actually barricades trauma in the energetic body. Within binary worldview, many of us rest in this deep state of energetic fatigue: under-valuing our agency, and losing contact with the divine spark of our humanness.

The Oblivious Blamer: Someone who selectively uses Destiny to absolve personal responsibility—like "blaming" certain outcomes on seemingly unchangeable parts of themselves or their environment. A simple, oft-heard example is: "Where are all the good men? I'm single because men suck." Often, with an inflated internal sense of self, the blamer looks outside of themselves—griping about the "unchangeable" context of their surroundings, and repackaging Destiny as a "that's just the way it is" worldview. In this throw-the-inner-arms-up mentality, we unknowingly give up the personal power we need to shift the way in which we are interpreting a situation or our environment.

The Spiritual Sociopath: Someone who uses Self-Will alone to try and "change" outcomes. Some strands of modern, commercialized spirituality give us the impression that adopting the right mindset and working harder at mastering our Self-Will will create a picture-perfect life. This, in turn, leads us to "pimp out" our Self-Will in an extractive manner—engaging in a self-obsessed way of using our will to "manifest" what we want. This keeps the Spiritual Sociopath from fully participating in a co-creative relationship with surrounding forces, their own and other people's divine skill sets, and universal energies.

In the above archetypes, excess Self-Will might give the facade of empowerment, but in the long run this approach will cause deep "Self-Will fatigue" where we hit a glass ceiling in our spiritual transformation and self-identity evolution. Many students find me right at this juncture in their lives: through Self-Will alone they have made so many life changes that things appear to be lining up. They are surface level "happy," and yet there is a deeper yearning to feel a more fully exalted sense of their human potential in collaboration with self, community, and culture: their Dharma.

And at the other end, binary Destiny often denies us access into the complexity of our personal meta-dialogue, and the many energetic narratives at play in a given situation—and thus, denies us access to the many moments when we can tactfully act to affect both our personal story and the environment we inhabit. The students I see polarizing here are often left with passionless, fake smiles of acceptance plastered on their faces. Diminished personal power and a submission to Destiny or limited definitions of God leaves them never truly knowing their unique karmic skill set and its potent work in the world.

Within binary worldview, Karma is often talked about in punitive, cause and effect terms. It is seen as either something to be "fixed" through Self-Will in order to develop "better" Karma, or as something to submit to completely through Destiny. We feel exhausted by the parts of ourselves we don't like but feel that we cannot change. And Dharma, in turn, is seen as either a "role" or material world occupation that we can forcibly uncover through Self-Will, or an abstract, Destiny-divined purpose that martyrs itself to the universal without any personal specificity.

But when we work to break the Self-Will/Destiny binary, we are able to access personal Karma as our unique "imprint"—a part of our conscious and unconscious identity that asks us to both accept our limitations and use them to hone our personal skill set. Rather than holding a negative or a positive charge, Karma simply holds the directly proportional consequence to a given action, honoring all of the causes and conditions that give rise to and motivate this action. In turn, acceptance and honing of our karmic imprint lets us access Dharma: our fully-exalted collaborative potential that places this subtle body imprint into a universal context. Tactful awareness of our Karma, in unison with action that accepts the effects of our past actions, leads to our sustainable path of service: our Dharma.

Operating from either side of the Self-Will/Destiny binary denies each one of us from realizing our overarching skill set, which we can apply in alignment with a personal vision that serves communal transformation. In this chapter, we will cultivate sensitivity around our own Karma and how it becomes a spoke in the wheel of Dharma—exploring how to use our creative life force to co-create with the Universe through humility and service.

In the coming sections, we will deeply explore the myths around Karma and outline the three types of Karma that play a role in understanding personal skillful action out in the world. Then, we will dive into our Personal Inquiry Practice, working with our natal charts to understand both our patterning and the agency we have available within our own unique path to live a life of service for ourselves, others, and our community. Finally, we'll be ready to break the binary, exploring Dharma and the true meaning of reciprocal, sustainable service through the exaltation of our current incarnation's unique energetic skill set.

THE MYTHS OF SELF-WILL/DESTINY

The Good Karma Myth
Good things happen to good people
They really have it coming
My Karma made me do it

These binary understandings of Karma place Self-Will at the center of a universe where we believe we can make changes to change an outcome—but where we are ultimately inhabitants of a scary and potentially punitive place where past actions decide our Destiny.

Embedded in this thinking is a punishing Godhead who will either give or take away, and a predestined sense of "God's plan." Destiny becomes a destination that we reach through the grace of God, and Self-Will becomes an arm of the capitalist structure that tells us working harder and suffering more is what brings rewards. "Good Karma" is the result of struggle, hardship, restraint, and self-punishment.

In this binary worldview, we see a punishment/reward behavioral model, where we put in the effort of "good" behavior in order to "get paid" a certain outcome from the universal ATM. We believe that we have the agency to create different outcomes, but we are always waiting for the other shoe to drop. No matter how hard we work at being good, we never know if it's enough for things to turn out golden—or exactly how the big old scary Universe will punish or reward us based on our behavior.

In this model, our Self-Will isn't actually "free" because we're stuck within a locked system. We believe it is within our power to rise up and change our Destiny at any moment, and also that we must struggle and fight to prove that we are worthy of Destiny's even grander plan. We're simultaneously too big and too small, keeping ourselves from enacting a right-sized, co-creative relationship with all of the forces that live within us and around us.

This binary worldview also springs from and perpetuates a limited understanding of cause/effect: we see Karma as something fated, but on which our actions have impact. This positions us as egoic "subjects," who can either act or be acted upon by external forces, rather than equal participants in a cycle that exists within us and is created through us.

But in non-binary worldview, THERE IS NO SUCH THING AS GOOD AND BAD KARMA. The root of the word Karma is "kr," which means to act or to be active, and speaks to the transformative energies of movement and action. Within its original Hindu and Buddhist context, there is an impersonal aspect to Karma; the entire universe is a series of cycles, and the nature of any one cycle is to move, flow, change, and always be in a state of "play" or "flux." What is present in a state of flux? Constant movement, constant action. And not always Self-Will motivated action; instead, the root "kr" refers to *constant universal action that is unbound from egoic identity.*

Karma is not something that happens to us; rather, it is a cycle that IS US!

When we operate from binary Self-Will, we believe that we can predict the chain of causes, conditions, and effects that arises from the application of our efforts. But within a deeper understanding of Karma, this cause/effect chain moves in many directions simultaneously, and on many levels of consciousness. To observe the many layers of our Karma, we must first decenter egoic Self-Will.

I often like to visualize the complex web of creative combustion that is Karma as a pool table: a series of actions and interactions is always in play, and the role of Self-Will is one of adaptively learning how to use the context of the game to become increasingly clear about which next action to take. This takes us beyond cause and effect as a linear transaction between a subject and an object—where we commit an act and then the "Karma police" either punishes or rewards us. Instead, we connect with our creative force that is always constantly evolving.

Developing awareness around the many layers of our personal karmic pool table begins to unlock our own psychic sensitivities; we come to know our own Karma so deeply that we are no longer limited by it.

The Self-Improvement Myth

As defined in the Upanishads, the first layer of Karma—Prarabdha Karma—is the ripening of previously planted fruits that are coming to unchangeable fruition in our current incarnation.

Examples of Prarabdha Karma include:

Our family units, or lack thereof, and the situation we were born into
Our upper limits of mental and physical performance
Our genetics and physical attributes
Our astrological signatures—the exact stellar situation in which we entered the world

What do we do with the parts of our unchangeable nature that we deem unfair, undesirable, intolerable, or unlovable? In binary worldview, we often lean on excessive Self-Will, using our "personal power" to either hide away, hate on, or spend all our energy trying to "fix" or "change" these parts. Instead of accepting who we are, and bringing our skillful means to the social context in which we have reincarnated, we adopt a fatalist mentality of self-punishment, judgment, and even shame.

We see this in the countless self-improvement industries, which peddle everything from performance enhancing drugs to plastic surgery, and in the increasingly threatening developments of AI and its potential to interface with our biology. The sales pitch of better, faster, stronger, and more productive (and therefore happier), positions parts of the "ripe fruit" of our Prarabdha Karma as both undesirable and "fixable," which leads us to misuse our Self-Will in order to try and change them.

Within binary worldview, Self-Will fatigue arises because we see the unchangeable parts of ourselves as a burden. We resign all self-respon-sibility through a vision of Karma as being something "bad" that hap-pens to us. We simultaneously wear ourselves out trying to change the unchangeable instead of bringing awareness to how our negative bias to-wards these parts of ourselves affects our moment-to-moment responses. Self-Will becomes a form of self-abuse, and as we hyper-focus on what we see as the "negative" parts of ourselves (as defined by binary worldview), we become increasingly disempowered—feeling crushed by our life cir-cumstances as opposed to set in motion by them, and wasting our energy fighting a losing battle.

To truly evolve in line with our Dharma, we must accept full respon-sibility for the parts of our Karma that seem "unchangeable." It is only through self-intimacy that we can begin to utilize our Prarabdha Karma as a vehicle of consciousness transformation; not as something to fix or make better, but as an intimate road map to self-knowing.

Rather than being weighed down with self-loathing, we connect with feelings of levity and freedom as our spiritual sensitivity to the context of our existence (our karmic "pool table") becomes heightened. This process begins with *understanding that which you think you cannot change and accepting that side of you by giving it the proper context in which to shine!* This is a radical act of attention-filled action that mobilizes your unique karmic skill set.

From this place of self-knowledge and acceptance of our Prarabdha Karma, the second layer of Karma—Kriyaman Karma—becomes *right ac-tion*, given the personal, social, and political context. Intimacy with our own Karma, and our innate belief systems around this Karma, allows us to start to uncover the proper and potent contexts for these unique skill sets to be of service.

In non-binary worldview, we come to see our Prarabdha Karma as the raft and our Kriyaman Karma as the oar, steering us through the sea of cyclical action. Our strong and objective relationship to our unique kar-mic fruits is the teaching itself—the "haul" of our ship. There is no need for "self-improvement" here, but instead a shift in context that allows us to transmute what binary society deems the unchangeable, undesirable parts of the self. Shift the context, shift the form, shift along with Karma.

The Just Surrender Myth

Everything happens for a reason
Freedom comes from letting go
I just need to surrender

But "surrender" to what?

Your lack of awareness about how your karmic fruits are playing out in your life? The heavy emotion that arises from your mind's inability to come up with an answer? A universal scapegoat to blame for the fact your life isn't working? Within the Self-Will/Destiny binary, many of us come to believe that surrender is a passive, actionless state that necessitates giving up all Self-Will in favor of Destiny. This "everything happens for a reason" and blind surrender approach causes us to retreat into blame and absolve ourselves of responsibility for our actions and reactions. And this keeps us trapped in a powerless place devoid of true agency, unable to connect with the realms that exist beyond egoic explanation.

Oftentimes, when our rational mind struggles to know, define, or solidify an answer, we rush to the Destiny end of the binary, thereby bypassing creative collaboration with universal cycles. But, in "letting go and letting God," we actually keep ourselves from experiencing the numinous states of elevated awareness that exist beyond the mind, while falling asleep at the wheel of our action-oriented Kriyaman Karma. We also ignore that one of our key functions within this human incarnation, "kr," is to act—the very reason we all have karmic imprints to work through in this given life.

Adopting a non-binary approach means cultivating acceptance—skillful surrender—in relationship to our Prarabdha Karma, so we can utilize the power of kriyaman Karma—right action—to transmute the third type of Karma: Sanchita Karma. Though associated with the acceptance of reincarnation, Sanchita, loosely, means "stored": the cumulative essence of you that's been built up through conscious actions you've taken, contexts into which you were born, and the numinous realms of inheritance we sometimes touch into through "deja vu" moments. And its wisdom can be observed even if reincarnation is not a religious belief of your own.

Sanchita Karma says: *I can never know the true impact of my decisions or actions. But I can accept, study, and rigorously work with my Prarabdha Karma— that which seems unchangeable.* Through present moment Kriyaman Karma (right action), I have the power to transmute that which seems unchangeable through the context by which I view it and share it.

What happens for a reason?
My Prarabdha Karma: the unique parts of myself to which I must strengthen my relationship.

What do I surrender to?
The skillful means and right action of Kriyaman Karma, which responds in full, humble observation of the cyclical process, surrendering to both the reciprocity of my own actions and to all that I do not know.

Where do I apply Self-Will?
To developing attention around what is occurring and sensitivity to my role within it. For the yogi, this means mobilizing Self-Will through a daily practice of contemplative living, rather than a search for hard and fast answers.

Now, "surrender" is an act of aligned Self-Will that trains the attention to recognize the actions that co-create a path of personal fulfillment and communal service. New, right actions gently evolve our Sanchita Karma and the world begins to respond to what we've deemed "unchangeable" differently, because we are now intimately aware of and humbled to our own karmic pool table. Because the field of change has widened through a shifting gaze, we can become true tools of change.

THE 3 LEVELS OF KARMA

Uncovering your karmic structure is the path to understanding your many layers. These reference points, and how you choose to inter-act with them over the course of your life, is the "essence" of you.

Prarabdha Karma: the karmic situation that you were born into, which is unchangeable—birth parents, body, constitution, genes, and the undeniable fact that time is limited on earth in a human body.

Kriyaman Karma: the area of choice and the actions you are per-forming now. There is no power greater than right action using skill-ful means in the present moment.

Sanchita Karma: subtle body, stored Karma, both from other life-times and the residue from past actions and choices.

PERSONAL INQUIRY PRACTICE:
UNCOVERING KARMA THROUGH YOUR NATAL CHART

A realized being
Taps you on the shoulder
In the imagination of your
Body/Mind, this incarnation
They whisper

With soft yet stern words
"Close your eyes,
Tell me what you see,
When you imagine ...
Your Flourishing, as is

The world around you"
Go with skillful means
To every single end
To bring that vision
Into form ...

Over the years of working with individuals from all walks of life, I have found the astrological natal chart to be a potent entry point into understanding the karmic essence. Through studying this map of the heavens at the time we incarnated, we can begin to uncover our Prarabdha Karma. While we might not be able to change these more fixed karmic "attributes," with more personal intel about our tendencies, we can develop clear, loving communication about these parts of ourselves and can consciously choose actions (Kriyaman Karma) that harness these energies for their highest good, in service of shifting our Sanchita Karma and coming closer to our Dharma.

As we move through this astrological Personal Inquiry Practice, I challenge you to answer from your own point of view. Try not to Google, look up information from another source, or remember some interpretation you've read. For that reason, I will NOT instruct you to access your natal chart information for the first few steps of this inquiry. Answering from the reservoir of your heart will deepen your organic awareness of your own Karma before you seek outside input to interpret it.

If you don't immediately feel or know an answer, that's okay: you have entered into the land of contemplation. As philosopher and teacher Jiddu Krishnamurti says, "Observation is action." When you are engaged in actively observing yourself within certain situations, building personal awareness of your default settings, you are both uncovering Karma and dropping new karmic seeds.

Archetypal Inquiry
Before you're tempted to pull up your actual birth chart, begin by reflecting broadly on these chart placements and their meaning within your own body/mind.

The Sun: Values and Driving Desires

While we don't always show these intimate, driving forces to the world, this planet symbolizes what we see as valuable and fulfilling within our current karmic imprint.

Define your "lived value set." List your deepest driving desires that define your mission and who you are in the world. Move beyond just the physical realm in answering this question: dig deep into your emotions, your personal actions of integrity, and your personal ethics.

Chiron + Lilith: The Karmic Self-Sabotage That Prevents You From Stepping Into Your Dharma

These placements help us understand our stored, Sanchita Karma: the beliefs we've acquired during nurture and socialization in this incarnation and through past incarnations. Using these placements helps us get clear about our inner blindspots where resistance arises to consciousness expansion and ego-structure dissolution, so we can then initiate truly aligned, skillful change.

Chiron: With pointed focus, begin to ask yourself what insecurities or blockages prevent you from stepping fully into your communal service work in the world. Step one is to outline the details and shape of the communal service, love, and support you can offer to others. Step two is to clearly write out what emotions, situations, and life contexts currently prevent you from stepping cleanly into that role.

Lilith: The mindset piece of how/why our Chiron service work struggles to take shape, Lilith holds the internal secrets about how we feel, what we need, and the self-sabotaging ways we hold ourselves back that we wouldn't dream of telling someone else. Clearly outline the mindset shifts you would need to make on a daily basis to embody the sustainable out-in-the-world service work that is unique to your karmic imprint.

The Midheaven + The North Node: The Cosmic Venn Diagram of Karma + Dharma

These placements allow us to work actively with our Karma as we move towards our Dharma: both the path itself and the vehicle. Our Midheaven is the path that allows our Dharma to take the shape of fully exalted service in the world; and our North Node is the vehicle that keeps us connected to our service through daily checkpoints during this process of actualization.

Midheaven: Your dharmic wheel of sustenance and the "bullseye" of your current incarnation's karmic layers, the Midheaven placement gives you clear intel around the physical shape of your work out in the world. Take your time and allow this reflection to be a Venn diagram of what you love, the skills you have practiced and worked to master, and the skills you must cultivate to bring this unique path of service into the world. Dream big here, drop the "shoulds," celebrate your skills, and listen to that heart whisper!

North Node: The karmic "Wheel of Action"—the "how" of actualizing our Dharma—this placement governs the process itself. The daily choices you must honor with the Midheaven bullseye as the target. This can be a list of physical choices and emotional boundaries that are non-negotiables for you in order to feel solid, self-assured, and passionate about aligning with your work and service in the world.

After several deep-dives into the questions above, find out the zodiacal placement of your Sun, Chiron, Lilith, Midheaven, and North Node (you can either look up your whole chart for free on websites such as astro.com, or simply Google questions like "what's my Lilith sign" to find the answers). From here, use the sign resource guide below to explore both where you are in the process of karmic "ripening"—learning to bring greater awareness to that particular sign's energy—and how you can move towards the karmic ripeness of this sign's mature expression.

In essence, the natal chart is a karmic roadmap, pointing to all of our strengths, blindspots, and unique skill sets. But this cosmic intel is only

KARMIC RIPENING	SIGN	KARMIC RIPENESS
Frustration; anger; self-centeredness; blunt and one sided communication; feels limited and upset by the physical; erratic misuse of energy; overly confident and competitive use of ego	ARIES	Initiatory spark; committed, passionate, driven, focused; body oriented and appreciative of physical form; full of energy and fiercely protective of boundaries of self and others
Stubborn, slow moving, indecisive; too much in the head and not enough action; stagnates in attachments to the sensual; mothers other with "love," micromanaging mother vibe	TAURUS	Exalted caretaker of all that is beautiful; a steward of Earth with an appreciation for its processes; deep, sustaining nourishment through mastery of the material world
Scattered with thoughts, connections, and actions; an over-talker; does things with haste; struggles to identify and work through their own emotions; many sides to the personality	GEMINI	Adaptive, masterful communicator given the situation; deep understanding of communal energetics and underlying forces at play; visionary in personal and big picture thinking

Victimhood mentality; plays out the manipulative feminine characteristics; depression, self-harm; always seeks safety and can become addicted to comfort; lacks confidence; takes on the emotions of others very easily	CANCER	Psychic qualities, transformative empathy and deep states of feeling; intuitive self-nurturance; comes to the support of others with an open loving heart; maturity in healing masculine/feminine binary beliefs
Takes up too much space in public; needs to be the center of attention or chief "ideas person"; overtly social and always seeking attention and adoration; difficulty with energy containment; immature leadership	LEO	Heart centered courage; loyalty in love; space holding support and leadership with an open heart; a plan maker and a structure creator from this loving heart space; confident but also emotionally available
Addicted to perfectionism in relationship to self and surrounding environments; overscheduled micro-manager; has a hard time dealing with chance and uncertainty; has a deep need to be validated as always being "right"	VIRGO	The master of energetic containment and personal prana usage; sees into future events and knows how to arrange energy to get there; deep soul-felt service to help others create the context for personal growth

	LIBRA	
Decision paralysis and difficulty speaking up due to constant inner confusion and passiveness; meddling in others' issues under the guise of helpfulness; egoic desire to be seen as the "helpful" or "intellectual" one		Clear communication and action that assert justice in all forms; ability to see the Middle Path and help others find seamlessness within the human paradox; deep service to society in helpful ways
Has a mysterious quality that is not always used for transformation and can tend towards manipulation; obsessed with power dynamics and always hiding motives in secret; power is shiny and is immaturely worshiped	SCORPIO	Sees through darkness with precision and clarity; always feels the undertone of a situation; has the communication skills to handle destructive emotions in self and within group dynamics; master of sustainability within energy use
Hyper intellectual; forgets to tend to the sacredness of the physical realm; always outward facing and struggles with internal presence; loses authenticity of self in overzealous adoption of external teachings	SAGITTARIUS	Passionate and purpose driven with a clear, potent mindstream; accepts the process of the hero/heroine journey and walks the path with courage and an open heart; motivation is high and is always used with precision

	CAPRICORN	
Heavy handed and tends toward judgment; a bit of a stick in the mud who finds it hard to mobilize new ways of being, ideas, or change; addicted to routine or structure in an unforgiving way		Organizer of earthly projects, energy, and money; great at affirming others and keeping everything together to bring energy into form; practices deep discernment in where/how they give their time and effort
Scattered and has a hard time focusing on the task or issue at hand; over communicates to the point of exhaustion; detaches from intense emotions and leaves no time for personal integration or reflection	AQUARIUS	A unique creative genius that connects the right people, places, and needs at the right time; highly intelligent and knows when to trust intuition; holds ample space for all forms of human expression
No boundaries and lacks clear motivation; very passive and often is walked on by others; has difficulty processing emotions that feel all-consuming; overextends empathy, often leading to fatigue and burnout	PISCES	Fully exalted vision of the big picture; a well of compassion and acceptance for others; extremely creative and motivated by service, love, and community support; highly intuitive and knows how to protect energy

helpful if we place it in the realm of right action, shifting our behavior based on the new vantage points of self the chart affords us. Remember that the root "kr" means action; that all Karma is mutable, and that it evolves *through* us.

By engaging with this cosmic signature contemplative work, you are pulling all the karmic reference points in the sea of your subconscious to the surface of your awareness. Once we can clearly see the many layers of our cosmic essence, we can then begin to approach our Dharma with piercing clarity.

BREAKING THE BINARY: UNLOCKING YOUR MUKTI CODE

In binary worldview, we often hear Dharma defined as a highly individualistic "personal purpose" that leads to self-fulfillment. But in non-binary worldview, the wheel of Dharma and its root, *dhri*—which means to sustain, support, and uphold—has larger ethical implications in the world beyond how you make money, your job, or your role within your family unit, and acknowledges that our personal paths must also be filled with service that honors one another.

Moving towards this exalted form of Dharma means we must learn how to apply Self-Will with embodied knowledge; continually uncovering our karmic patterning, then taking present-moment actions to respond to this patterning with consciousness, then surrendering to the effects of our actions taken (along with the constant reverb from all actions taken in our lifetime by us, by other forces, and in previous incarnations). It is a dance of awareness, action, and adjustment. Using the above exercise, you built awareness of your natal chart patterning, so you could take more conscious actions within the context of your Prarabdha Karma—evolving through both your patterning and your personal willpower, within the larger cyclical dance of the Universe.

When we start to follow this approach, we're able to move beyond limiting states of Self-Will fatigue. And in this space, we can actualize our SvaDharma (Personal Dharma). We cultivate an understanding of

SvaDharma by asking ourselves questions like: *What is my inner nature? What is my deepest driving desire?* But then we must press further to understand how this fits into Universal Dharma and Cosmic Virtuous Law, asking: *Where do I find the most service within society?*

Our "Mukti Code" is a personal statement that assists us in making daily choices and creating boundaries in order to uphold this personal path and live in karmic/dharmic alignment: both meeting our needs while also considering the larger ecosystem as we search for our personal place. If SvaDharma is the energetic "transmission," then your Mukti Code is the golden standard that keeps the transmission intact. Your Mukti Code organizes your entire karmic constitution towards sustainable service, unifying the many roles you might play in this lifetime, and allowing you to assert Self-Will with both freedom and self-awareness, in the proper context. This personal self-organization principle allows each of us to fact check choices, people, opportunities, relationships, collaborations, and life events against the inner sustainable truth that we cultivated through uncovering our karmic blindspots.

Clarifying Your Mukti Code

Your Mukti Code is a one sentence statement that:

Supports a state of mind, a condition of body, and an evolutionary understanding of self that governs day-to-day action. This code focuses your efforts on creating a chain of cause and effect that allows for the actualization of a sustainable dreamstate, your SvaDharma.

Once we narrow down this self-sustaining statement, we can use it to measure all potential choices and actions that come our way. Let's zoom in on a few placements from our natal chart work to help us develop the lightning clarity and language contained in your Mukti Code:

Sun Sign Step

Look back at your Sun sign placement and focus on the mature, "ripe" aspects of your Karma within this sign. The language of your Mukti Code will need to connect you with these mature aspects in order to help you attain your deep driving desire through elevated action. Pay close attention to the "ripening" end of your Sun sign placement as well, ensuring that the language of your Code can catch that meta-dialogue demon by its leg.

Chiron Placement Step

Look back at your Chiron placement: what intel did it reveal to you about the public presence of your personal work of service out in the world? Does your Code support this evolutionary trajectory, no matter the physical situation?

Lilith Placement Step

This is how you can locate your own "suffering," tendency towards passiveness, and outsourcing of self-responsibility. Does the language of your Code speak directly to this insidious self-sabotage with loving awareness, so you always uproot the tendency to self-destruct when you contemplate the implications of your SvaDharma out in the world? This part of developing your Code can be deeply private and sacred as we often don't admit these tendencies, even within our most intimate relationships.

Midheaven Step

Look back at your Midheaven placement and explore the "ripening" and "ripe" aspects of that sign. This is the physical and tangible way to bring your SvaDharma to life through a job, a project, a role on a team, and your daily physical work flow, and how your personal Karma can thrive inside these physical project containers. List the energetic qualities many of these containers have in common and make sure that your Code speaks to the through-threads between them; you'll need to uphold this energetic essence in almost every life situation for your SvaDharma to thrive.

North Node Step

Look back at your North Node placement and highlight the most resonant intel that arose from your contemplation of it and the sign that it occupies. It is imperative that you make daily choices to meet the demands symbolized by this placement in order to reach the full exaltation of your karmic imprint. Outline what those demands are in bullet point form and make sure your Code speaks to them.

Informed by the inquiry of this entire section, your Mukti Code is one sentence of lightening clarity as to how your Karma informs your SvaDharma. It will speak to how you can use the skills you brought in to inform your larger, service-based purpose. If I were to tell you my Mukti Code it might not mean much, because it exists in reference to my deepest life's work. Your Mukti Code will feel this way as well: robust, resounding, chill-inspiring, and entirely personal. Your Code is yours and yours alone; rather than rushing to share it through social media's performative acts of vulnerability, keep it in the sacred vault of your own interpersonal dialogue. This statement holds the most motivational conviction if it retains your personal uniqueness and is respected as the door keeper to the sanctuary of living your SvaDharma.

It is the essence, the quality of being, and the guide in your actions that deeply SUSTAINS you.

Take the full month to dive into the practices in this chapter, honing your Mukti Code through the natal chart karmic uncovering inquiries, and with the support of the Meditation for Cosmic Stamina practice below. As you develop this Code, you will become less obsessed with asking self-willed questions like "what is my purpose," and more interested in how attention to your daily actions can naturally give rise to sustainable service.

Your Code will read as one golden statement that organizes your personal energy, decisions, and thoughts in the direction of dharmic alignment. Apply it regularly as a filter for your actions in the world, and your creative force (a non-binary understanding of Self-Will that takes into account the limitations of your karmic imprints) will align within the context of a co-creative universe (a non-binary understanding of Destiny through SvaDharma).

SUBTLE BODY PRACTICE

Meditation for Cosmic Stamina

Stamina is needed when committing to the karmic uncovering process in search of your SvaDharma. Because living with such authenticity is not always graciously accepted by the people and social structures around us, we'll need to be our own best friends and compassionate advocates. This practice is a booster shot for your consciousness expansion, which will help you develop the internal energetic stamina to dig deeply into your own programming and assert the skillful will to make changes, day-in and day-out.

Posture

Sit in Sukhasana, or a simple, cross-legged seat. Prop yourself, if necessary, to support your body. Make this easy on your posture and feel free to lean against something. If knee pain is present, you can always straighten your legs and support your lower back, or sit in a chair.

Mudra

Lift the arms, and clasp the hands by intertwining the fingers. The palms are face down towards the crown of the head. Slight bend in the elbows and the arms will create a mudra lock around the crown of the head.

Breath Pattern

Breathing is long, stable, and sustaining—in and out of the nose. A slight breath retention, a pause at the bottom of the inhalation and the exhalation, and repeat this long, stable pattern.

Timing

Practice 3 minutes daily for 30+ consecutive days.

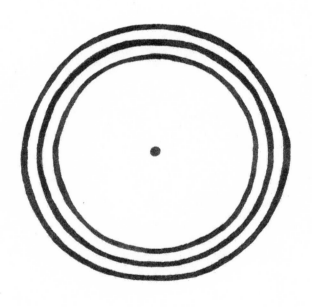

THE NINTH BINARY
PAST/FUTURE: CLAIRSENTIENCE

Quiet.

With eyes closed, the glory of the sun's morning rays through the window is felt as the sensation of warmth on the skin. Legs crossed, this posture is a dear old friend, worn with care. Drawing the senses inward to explore the vast landscape of perception. Feeling like a speck in the sea of it ALL. Expanding into vastness, boundaries of self, blurred.

Then, at the center of the Universe again, with pressing inner voices demanding attention. Flashes of judgment, labels, clinging to answers, needing validation. The seemingly segregated spaces of me; can you see? *Is it Me or We? How long have I been sitting here?* asks that familiar nagging voice. No response needed, quiet is the answer in itself.

The mind free falls down an elevator shaft for a moment. It fears having no external reference points for itself, so it struggles. It calls out into the void of the inner being because it fears becoming obsolete. Yet the void, this space beyond Time, holds it all. It feels like a room with padded walls, location unknown, temperature indiscernible, reflection non-existent. All of the fluctuation and agitation that moves across the surface of the being is laid to rest here. All of the "constructs" it deems constant go to die here.

As this realization settles beyond the language function, the ego-structure stops working so hard to locate itself through echolocation. A deafening quiet that has its own texture. The ear canals are turned inward, the pumping of veins so loud that the rhythm connects you to a larger hum. Eyes closed, in this imageless space there is no single place to fixate consciousness; no anthropomorphized reflection. Intel streaming in from all angles and territories of existence. A flashback, a flash forward, unrecognizable to the default mode settings of comprehension.

There is no "doing" here, only to be undone.

Then, the wind of the inhalation registers on the monitor of the medulla, and that blip on the radar agitates the default mode network. It quickly asserts its limits, as if they are the totality of reality. A sense of self—rooted in illusionary continuity based on a perceived timeline of events—returns.

Thoughts, images, memories, and identity recognition come rushing in. *Who am I?* So quickly, so bright, so attention-grabbing is the response, that it plucks you from the ubiquitous sea and returns you to the construct of you. You're back on the clock.

... exhalation.

The most stubborn psychological concept that exists, our ego-structure's understanding of Time, and the Past/Future binary that perpetuates it, is the greatest and most insidious threat to our true creative nature. When we rigidly locate ourselves within the Past/Future binary, it sounds like:

By this age I will be doing ...
By this age I must have ...
By this age I will be feeling like ...

I can't believe this is still lingering, I should be over this by now ...
Uhhhhhh, why haven't I figured this out yet? I am already in my 40s ...
That's just the way it's always been ...

Within binary worldview, Time is a mechanism of measurement that we use to build expectations about our identities and the world. And when we live within this binary, we forget that self-transformation doesn't happen along a socially constructed timeline.

232

At the Past end of the binary, we can feel "trapped," wishing we could go "back in time" to change or alter our circumstances, and limiting our sense of possibility in the present based on our perception of what's come before. And at the Future end of the binary, we're often driven forward by "ideal" visions of self and goals we would like to attain, while simultaneously projecting fear and anxiety onto an unknown future. As we constantly strive towards the Future from a place of constant self-improvement, attachment to the Past/Future binary leaves an intense weight on our body/mind.

In the Past/Future binary, we organize our entire linear understanding of the Universe within a supposedly forward-moving trajectory: away from the Past and towards the Future. Yet everything we do, say, and think, encodes space itself with information—information that exists in perpetuity. Even if, to our continuous concept of self, it seems that it is either lost to the Past or a projection into the Future.

Our memories of the Past are not as linear as we perceive them to be; nor is our movement into a perceived Future. Instead, our perception of the present is the result of repeated neural wiring in response to events we have experienced. This means each Past event exists continuously as both the lens through which we meet the present, and the telescope with which we look to the Future. Because the Past is more easily revisited in our human memory hardware, this results in a constant projection of what we think we "know" onto the Future.

This process of limited perception is what I term the "Associative Architecture" of the body/mind. A prevalent concept in Thervada Buddhist texts long before the modern advent of neuroscience, our Associative Architecture describes the field of consciousness that our binaried self sees as "reality." Each event we experience creates chemical, neurological residue in our body/mind's hardware, and this residue causes us to look at present and future events to find what is recognizable, rather than to be available for newness. The result? A limited version of self and our life's possibilities that is bound to what we think we've "been" and, therefore, what we can "become."

When we get hooked into the Associative Architecture of the Past/

Future binary, we forget that each moment of our lives is an unreplicable juncture in space, which offers infinite potentials and experiences—some of which cannot be measured through linear means. The Past/Future's illusionary sense of linearity can feel so real at any even given juncture; yet it obstructs our ability to receive intel from the vast sea of infinite consciousness itself. If we stay immersed in this binary and its measurement of Time, we lose access to the mystical, spiritual, extraterrestrial realms of intel that come to us through our faculties of subtle perception.

Breaking this binary means recovering access to our "Clairsentience": an expanded understanding of "intuition." While intuition is sometimes understood as a way to make future decisions, Clairsentience is a 360-degree awareness of the many layers of consciousness that exist beyond our identification with a continuous self that moves from the Past and into the Future. This multifaceted intel might not always be what you *want* to see, hear, or know in order to wrap up the Past or divine in which direction to head next.

Cultivating Clairsentience requires us to intimately understand how our "personal" ego-structure filters "impersonal," universal data. After peeling back layer upon layer of this dense societal and self-programming and fixed identity, we now stand poised to enter a timeless relationship with the quantum field of all possibilities, allowing the many layers of truth to emerge within us and around us through a sensing of energy movement at any given juncture. I'm using the word "juncture" here to move us beyond the landscape of Time and towards a limitless, timeless space that contains all possibilities and all limitations simultaneously: beyond labels, beyond constructed timelines, and even beyond the fallacy of the "present moment."

Breaking this binary requires a psychological willingness to keep questioning "reality" and opening further to your limitless aliveness. This doesn't mean that you will bypass or not come to terms with your Past and your generational imprint, or that you are not allowed to have Future goals and visions. You will still wake up to your alarm clock, you will still see the sun set—and on one level these demonstrate the physical passing of Time. But through questioning the psychological and cultural imprints of "time constructs" upon our self-identity, we can begin to access the exalted portals of Clairsentience. These portals move us from "I" consciousness and towards a more receptive quality of consciousness that senses greater possibilities in all directions.

We need to dismantle many energetic layers of belief before we can authentically and openly address the cage of the Past/Future binary. If you hear or feel the ego-structure's musings of disbelief as I ask you to question reality itself, this is a clear indicator that other binaried formations are still occupying precious real estate in your inner being. It is courageous to acknowledge this with self-honesty; stay engaged by referencing the lines of contemplation from the previous Breaking the Binary sections of this book.

Alright, hold on as you step into the spacesuit of your flesh sack and learn to live in complete AWE for the unreplicable junctures you're passing through, and for the limitless being that you are.

THE MYTHS OF PAST/FUTURE

The Be Present Myth
All we have is this moment
Breathe into the Now
True power is in the present

The power of connecting with "the now" can have profound effects on our ability to become aware of our emotional states and central nervous system fluctuations. Yet, when we get mired in simplistic notions of "presence," we often stay caught in the cage of the Past/Future binary. We are not taking in the totality of what is happening within us and around us at all times. Instead, we are still seeing the present through the landscape of the ego-structure and missing out on the complexity of the juncture at hand and the many threads of consciousness coming together.

In neuroscientist Steven Johnson's *Mind Wide Open*, he underlines that memories can trigger emotional loops that directly affect what we call the

235

"present moment." In short, it doesn't matter whether we're being triggered by the actual event at hand, or a recollection it brings forth. Further, he states that reactivating memories in a new context can actually change the trace of the memory itself. So if the body/mind isn't as adept as we believe it to be at differentiating between something that previously happened to us, and what is currently occurring, how can we train the attention to locate itself within a uniquely unfolding context, millisecond by millisecond?

This power lies in breaking the bonds of your Associative Architecture. By beginning to investigate how quickly our ego-structure likes to assert its outdated opinion—looking at where we're triggered in the present by an overwhelming memory, or where we project a Past version of self into the Future—our perception becomes more sensitive and our current situation is no longer defined by the chemical, physical, or memory imprints of the Past.

When we overuse the statement "be present," we are still attempting to "locate" ourselves through the lens of ego-structure. Completely transcending our ego-structure's locational ability altogether is not the answer to tapping into the deep intimacy of this moment, either. Instead, we must work to bear witness to the many layers of consciousness, keeping one foot in the "personal" camp, in order to hear the ego's inner workings; and one foot in the impersonal camp, listening to the multilayers of intel arising within the juncture. Thus, a moment in time can be informed by the Past without having to be defined or unconsciously created by it.

When we start to examine all of the threads that come together to form the "now," we begin to question what is "real" and this questioning gives us access to the gifts of timelessness: more intimacy with both the transitory and continuous parts of ourselves and our lives, and greater growth towards a fuller expression of self.

The altered states of consciousness that can move us closer to this sense of timelessness are often demonized by a capitalist, power-hungry society that values linear progress: less creativity means less rebellion and less personal agency. These alternate states of consciousness remain an integral part of life among many indigenous cultures, and as we reckon with the erasure done by extractive capitalism and seek to repair the violence it's caused, we have much to learn from this approach.

These experiences are sometimes classified as mystical experiences, ego deaths, or dissolutions into the divine. When we get curious about these kinds of experiences and question the "normal," we can begin to undo the Past/Future binary's assumptions about who we are, where we are, and where we're heading.

These timeless experiences of an alternative "present" are often associated with plant medicines and mind-altering substances. But the first time I had one of these experiences, I was in the middle of the woods in British Columbia during a six-hour walking meditation practice during which I consumed no substances. Very deep into the meditation, I remember my rate of perception speeding up very quickly, as if I was in some sort of "light tunnel." Images of constellation pathways raced through my field of perception. Yet I could still feel my body walking, my arms swinging with each step. I dropped to my knees and shouted, "Who's going to yell 'cut'?! Who's going to tear down the back drop?!"

At that juncture, the world as I knew it became nothing more than a simulation, as my body/mind started to question reality and the notion of a continuous sense of self that is dependent on Time. To the casual onlooker, it might have appeared that I had entered a state of psychosis. The majority of us are untrained in how to acknowledge and integrate alternate states of consciousness. But this encounter with the world behind the curtain was so profound for me that I recreated this walking mediation for years in different contexts to work with the limitations of my own Associative Architecture.

In short, you exist far beyond the "present" dear one, forever leaving imprints, fractals, and frequencies in space.

Even though we appear to be separate entities—as a result of the self-imposed limits of our Associative Architecture—there exists an expanded, felt sense that our energy fields are enmeshed with everything that surrounds us. In deep realms of yoga philosophy and subtle body anatomy, this is called "transmission": the essence of what radiates from one's being, central nervous system, and auric field; the unspoken wordless energy exchange from entity to entity. As you begin to develop sensitivity within this intelligible space of enmeshed connection, you'll start to ask questions like:

To what am I being "present"? The information of the material world? The supposed appearance of others? My own inner state?

How can I acknowledge all of these things while also opening up to a more heightened, subtle awareness of wordless communication and transmission?

When we start to open in this way, we step out of our Associative Architecture as the total picture of reality. We begin to notice that it is only the gaze of perception that differentiates what has happened in the so-called "Past" from what might occur in the apparent "Future." This gives us the felt sense that the Past, present, and Future weave together into a cohesive field of awareness.

Many students I encounter seek intel on how to expand this felt sense of awareness to help move them beyond the ego-structure and the Past/Future binary, and "intuition" is often a word that's used to describe this sense. Yet we often get caught up in the egoic aspects of this process, mistaking intel from our personal reality as all that exists in a given situation, and using it as something to impress upon others simply because we've labeled it as "intuition."

When actually there are many voices and layers of intel that come together at each juncture in the present. In the Personal Inquiry Practice and Breaking the Binary sections that follow, we'll cultivate potent discernment around both how our "personal" Associative Architecture is constructed—and the limits therein—and how we can blend our knowledge of this personal architecture with "impersonal" intel in order to access a more limitless perception of both Time and self.

The Time Heals Myth

How do I parent my child so they do not absorb the same intergenerational pain that I did?
How do I forgive a past lover who deeply hurt me?
How do I "let go" of ... (insert your own narrative here)

As we try to make sense of the fragmented pieces of our lives, the words "trauma" and "intergenerational trauma" often come up. And while these are certainly valuable concepts, we often imbue them with an implicit negative bias that has us believe we must heal past "wrongs," or attempt to tie up our history with a bow in order to evolve and move forward.

As a young spiritual seeker in closed retreat for months on end, I kept getting clear, impersonal messages while in meditation to "explore your bloodline": the living conditions and relationships of those who birthed you and who birthed your parents; your understanding of nurturance; and your own perspective of the Past. What did your relatives eat? Where did they live? How did they treat each other? And how did you become the series of causes and conditions that you seem to recognize as your "self"?

I embarked on a body/mind inquiry that involved both meditation and neuroscience study, exploring the malleable shades of memory and shifting my understanding and recollection of the Past through active inquiry. I was lucky enough to have had direct contact with grandparents and great grandparents in my childhood and adolescence, so I had memories of my bloodline in the flesh, however inaccurate.

My self-guided methodology involved making lists of everything I remembered that spanned the good/bad binary: the positive/negative attributes of both my parents; the positive/negative relationship attributes between my parents and their parents. Through this process, I gained a balanced ability to assess intergenerational programming and a sense of how quickly one can change their understanding of self if they are free from the sticky bonds of what we so often deem the unchangeable Past.

For example, my extended family is very conservative, and hyper-masculinity was always celebrated and rewarded. As a female-bodied child, I pushed so hard to emulate these hyper-masculine qualities. When I started to sort through this inheritance without forcibly categorizing it as "good" or "bad," this veneration of the hyper-masculine that existed in my lineage naturally began to fall away from my own behavior, and a more sensitive, intuitive way of existing naturally rose to the surface. I began to notice an open willingness to forgive that came from a place of empowered understanding in relationship to my bloodline Karma: shorthand for the Prarabdha and Sanchita Karma we explored in the Eighth Binary. I was rewriting my own generational inheritance.

I call this tapestry of information, reflection, and understanding, Intergenerational Osmosis. When we shift the consciousness structure in this way, we don't just go in search of "trauma," but rather seek a full and total picture of the causes and conditions that gave rise to our own ego-structure.

This is not to deny painful and violent events that exist within our bloodline Karma. Many students and clients come to me after they have done extensive clinical work in coping with trauma and this clinical work creates massive progress in their personal healing. Yet while they feel like they can "own" their Past and clearly speak about their trauma, there is still an insidious energetic imprint that keeps them from developing a fully expressed openness towards and passion for a Future vision.

This Intergenerational Osmosis practice asks us to move beyond the notion that we must work to "fix" or "heal" the Past, and instead asks us to explore our Associative Architecture; developing a clear and transparent understanding that the Past is fully alive within our tissues, and that by acknowledging this, we can access the malleability of both our self and Time itself.

Epigenetics research is uncovering that the transmission of intergenerational trauma happens right down to the level of our DNA. As if the present is actually a semipermeable membrane, where past recollection, triggered emotion, and perception that is chemically influenced by the interplay of external stimulus interface with our genetic code. This multilayered experience is undeniably linked to those who predated us. Our predecessors may have experienced disease, despair, and unfavorable traumatic events in the intergenerational line. We (in the biggest sense of We) have the ability to alter perception with potent awareness, shifting the intergenerational trajectory for those who follow us through our different pathways of action, language function, lifestyle choices, and focus on community wellness.

How to "heal" the past?

We cannot shift our own transmission until we fully and wholeheartedly acknowledge that our perception of the Past is alive and well within us, deep in our cellular structure. By first giving the totality of your lineage a place to live within you, you can then begin to work with it in your lived experience.

Through active meditative inquiry, we can alter the expression of our structural inheritance with every thought, perception, and action we take. Step one is to give the analytical mind a task, beginning with the Intergenerational Osmosis process outlined above. The positive and negative columns will eventually collapse into one another, and you will start redefining your relationship to the living past within you. Acknowledgement of our "living past" moves us beyond our Associative Architecture of perception, leaving us with a limitless sense of the possibilities that can unfold.

And so you see, Time itself doesn't heal. YOU HEAL THE FUTURE by deeply learning from how your current perception of the Past is causing unconscious imprints onto the transmission of YOU.

The Age Appropriate Myth
You are so mature for your age.
You look so great for your age.
Age is nothing but a number.

Whether it's preconceptions about our bodies, or the achievement of cultural milestones, age is one of the immediate measurements by which we draw conclusions about another person's life experience, maturity, physical health, level of responsibility, and overall life status. And in the process of doing so, we often forgo the development of our own emotional

241

intelligence, stunting our self-concepts and internal perceptions through external barriers we impose based on a number.

This ageist regimentation starts in childhood through upbringing and the educational process, where metrics of development are often based solely on age, without consideration for other sets of behavior and elevated senses—which are especially important to cultivate before our neuroplasticity has hardened.

Ironically, we often say we "mature" with age and life experience, and yet our body/minds become *less* malleable, our views on reality more fixed, and our psychological adaptability more concrete-like. I started teaching when I was nineteen years of age and am writing this book at the chronological age of thirty-four. Throughout this time, the chronological age of many of my students has been five, 10, or 15 years older than me. It wasn't my age or therefore projected life experience that qualified me as their guide; instead, it was my commitment to creating a timeless connection to the intel of our consciousness.

On the flip-side, many consumer industries are dedicated to chasing youth, while getting chronologically older carries many negative implications. We certainly cannot deny the death of the physical body. But, if we are willing to question the implications of chronological age and its influence on our ego-structures, we keep our senses open to the other streams of consciousness we might have access to at any given juncture, giving rise to timeless qualities of the self.

Epigenetic research shows us that through thought processes, lifestyle choices, toxic exposure, and transgenerational inheritance, certain genes are turned on and off, and that these genes also affect generations to come. This groundbreaking information is not meant to spark self-punishment if we feel we aren't making "good" choices. Instead, paying attention to the variables over which we do have control on a daily basis can help us take full responsibility for our process of aging. Much like our discussion of Karma/Dharma, we find that DNA is not destiny, nor is our chronological age always an accurate measure of physical and emotional development.

Taking empowered responsibility for our limited experience of this physical body stands in stark contrast to the consumer-based anti-aging race against Time. As we learn to see ourselves as participants in a web of interconnection, right down to our genetic codes, we're no longer immersed in a losing battle against our failing bodies and fear of our inevitable demise. Instead, new doors of self-realization in the physical, emotional, and spiritual realms open to us. This shift empowers us to use our limited time on earth to create change within our karmic structure, and thus move beyond the rigid sense that we are defined by our "aging" bodies and closer to our Dharma, which serves both ourselves and the collective.

Our choices make changes not just in our genetic code, but in the cultural DNA of humanity: the "epigenome." What if we looked at our passage through this life as an opportunity to give more care and respect to one another; choosing to spend our limited time laying down chemical empathy, compassion, and emotional equilibrium that will affect generations to come?

PERSONAL INQUIRY PRACTICE: EXPLORING YOUR ASSOCIATIVE ARCHITECTURE

It has a hold
No matter which way I turn
My alarm clock
Still rings in the morning
I see the sun set

With my own eyes
Is that not the passing of time?
I mark my entire existence
By this passing
A unit of measure I mistake

For the limitlessness of my
Omnipresent self

Can reality shift

By merely keeping a question ALIVE?

Would rigidity go to die?

Would the "I"?

Over the course of this book, we have moved through a Consciousness Design Process that has asked you to cultivate the resilient ability to question "reality" on the deepest levels. And we've strategically left the stickiest binary for last! You are now ready to explore the "No-Self Doctrine"—a profound concept derived from Buddhist teachings that asks us to question the most embedded personal and cultural beliefs we use to make sense of the world. This dharmic concept presents the idea that our personal suffering arises from the notion of a "continuous self," or even an unchanging soul.

Within the Past/Future binary, we create a continuous version of self and superimpose this deeply held belief about "who we are" onto all life experiences and phenomena. This continuous self is not without its value, as it creates the psycho social sphere of interaction and an ability to engage within this shared reality. But when we see this version of self as the only possible reality available to us, we also buy into a continuous timeline that causes us to lose touch with other measurements for giving ourselves and our lives value. This not only affects how we perceive our self and others, but also how we connect to the world at large. The more tightly we associate our self-identities with the physical, material, and measurable constructs of Time, the more we end up spiritually dissatisfied—forgetting to equally value the phenomena that exists beyond logic, and denying the Earth's mystical sacredness.

The simple lines of inquiry below will help you to understand the limitations of your Associative Architecture and its rigid construction of a continuous version of self. From this point of understanding, you'll be ready to break the linear continuity of the Past/Future binary, braiding together the "personal" sense of continuous self, and the "impersonal" of No-Self.

1) *Write out three separate profound events that shifted the course of your life.*

These events can span the positive/negative binary. Select events that can feel unexplainable by logic. Or perhaps events that feel very real in your present moment tissues. Describe three of these "Past" events in great detail. Get all of your senses involved as you recall these three different events that have truly shaped your current identity.

2) *After you have these short, masterful reflections in all of their own focused detail, describe "the person you were" during each event.* Describe your self-image, your inner beliefs, and anything you can remember about your worldview: assumptions about self/others, or moments you still cling to in which you desire forgiveness for self/others. This line of inquiry can be very emotional, and is more about how you define yourself in relationship to each of those events.

3) *With complete honesty, place your awareness in the current iteration of your self-identity and life context.* Write out in detail all the ways you have changed and, on the other hand, the ways in which you might feel deep stagnation around the reconciliation of these memories. This reflection might not flow as easily as the prompts above. This is a cross referencing practice that will help you prove to yourself that the Past/Future binary's unchanging continuous version of self is malleable, and that change is the only constant.

Get creative, expressive, and emotionally transparent with yourself, choosing some of your most life altering memories and iterations of self to examine in this three-step reflection process. If we are at all curious about developing elevated senses, and portals to understanding different planes of reality, we need to question the root system that keeps us tethered to the Past/Future's superimposition of the continuous self.

When we question Time itself, big internal shifts and unpredictable moments can occur, as even what we thought of as pure FACT becomes an area for questioning. This is the precise purpose of the No-Self Doctrine: to examine the units of measurement by which we define reality and what we deem to be "true," and to be willing to exist in a space that contains NO ANSWER. Take care with these inquiries, ideally engaging in them with a loving and trusted partner who can be your sounding board as you dive in.

BREAKING THE BINARY: CLAIRSENTIENCE

After examining your personal Associative Architecture and starting to probe the limitations of a continuous self, you're ready to begin opening up to the many threads that are coming together to form this current juncture.

Defined as the ability to perceive that which is not usually, or normally, perceptible, embodying Clairsentience reminds us of the profound, jaw-dropping, multi-layered reality that we always have access to, and which exists within altered states of consciousness. Rather than linear measurements of progress, Clairsentience relies on the potency of our attention: a piercing ability to see beyond the mundane and into the many layers of intel streaming at any given juncture. Embodying Clairsentience is an ongoing, life-long practice, and it starts with learning to sense the distinction between the "personal" and "impersonal" intel that flows through us at each juncture.

I developed the practice below with an inquisitive student of mine who found herself deep in the realms of uncovering her Karma, examining her relationship to her bloodline through Intergenerational Osmosis, and expanding her sensitivity to all of the intel available beyond her Associative Architecture.

As we searched and reflected, we began to explore the Vedic concepts of Cit and Citta (pronounced "chit" and "chitta"). Loosely translated, Citta connects us to the realm of the "personal" and its many layers of ego-structure, while Cit brings us closer to the "impersonal" sound of cosmic consciousness. In identifying the distinction between these two concepts, she was able to shift from purely personal sound currents—bound by the ego-structure's Associative Architecture of the Past/Future binary—and into the elevated, impersonal sense portals of Clairsentience.

The consciousness shifting exercise below helps us cultivate a quality of expansive listening and receiving; as we learn to pay attention to the personal fluctuations of our Citta, we allow the more impersonal, expansive sound current of Cit to drop into our field. Sound creates structures within space, and while this listening practice might seem simple, when done with relentless attention, devotion, and authenticity it can open our realms of perception to hear "noise" that exists beyond the fluctuations of personal consciousness.

Information travels faster than our material sense portals can process. Therefore, make this journal extremely interactive. I carried around a tape recorder for years, so I could record spoken words. If you would like to write, that is fine too. Just ensure that this Expansive Listening Journal travels everywhere with you, so you can keep pace with changing concepts of self and Time as you prime your neural wiring to listen beyond the Past/Future binary.

Your Expansive Listening Journal

You will need two lines of inquiry paralleling each other at all times. Sometimes, in spoken word or writing, I ask students to refer to themselves in third person so they can differentiate the personal ego-structure and the Associative Architecture of Citta from the impersonal tone of Cit.

This is not a technique in which you sit down and "try" to hear the musings of the impersonal sound currents; it is a meditative quality of mind that moves about with you as you prime the space for Clairsentience to take shape.

In reference to any given juncture where you find yourself, record your stream of consciousness responses to the following prompts: I SEE, I FEEL, and I HEAR. Denote that these meta-dialogue musings are your personal sound current.

Record the musings of an impersonal sound in the same manner. I SEE. I FEEL. I HEAR. The impersonal will sound nothing like you, and you will notice when "you" are trying to "notice something." Keep reflecting your creativity into the sea of Cit. I SEE. I FEEL. I HEAR.

As you begin this process, don't worry if you feel like you're not hearing anything discernable at all. This is simply because you are so inundated with your own personal Citta, your meta-dialogue. Simply keep attuning to the elevated senses of Clairsentience with love, attention, and devotion, multiple times a day. Remember that beautiful quote that states "observation is action" and continue to listen—opening your exalted senses to hear both the personal and the impersonal sounds and vibrations, as you move towards a more limitless, elevated measurement of the timelessness of space.

The result? Through listening for the impersonal movements of Cit, we begin to glimpse the No-Self as a possibility. This takes us far beyond the usual conversations about "selflessness," which can actually be quite selfish, as they still reference a self-concept that plays with the realms of ego and the personal. The realm of self-less-ness we're exploring here is the doorway to Clairsentience: access to the universal realm of elevated perception and limitless creativity. Through this contemplation, we no longer confine the idea of our existence to something that's "our own," or even continuous within itself through Time. Instead, our existence becomes a series of causes and conditions, and we begin to understand our "personal self" as cohesively connected to all rising and falling phenomena.

Time is certainly a unit of measurement around which to organize these phenomena. But every unit of measurement has its glass ceiling and limiting factors. An embodied non-binary worldview is one in which every single unit by which we measure existence is run through the gauntlet of contemplation—giving us access to impersonal intel which exists beyond binaried thought. In a world in which we cling to a binary reality, developing a resilient, balanced central nervous system that can rest in the space of No Answers *is* the process of elevating our senses beyond the Past/Future binary and into Clairsentience.

Over the course of this book, we have strategically organized, examined, and created awareness around the many binaried concepts that build our "continuous" sense of self. And you've now reached the point in the process where breaking the binaries within you is leading you towards your non-binary Transitory Nature. No longer defined by opposing forces that seek to limit and repress, from here you can draw from your own living, fresh empirical data, and use it to stay connected within a web of cosmic causality that exists behind and beyond the continuous self. There is NO CONCLUSION—no Future end point to be reached; the process itself holds it ALL.

SUBTLE BODY PRACTICE
Decoding Memories + The Dissolution of the Self

This consciousness altering practice was gifted to me during my time at Yasodhara Ashram, founded by Swami Radha. This walking meditation is an incredible practice that allows "past perception" memories to come to the surface of our consciousness awareness. As we develop an ability to replay and restructure the "living past," we have an opportunity to change the chemical and neurological landscape of "who we think we are."

This practice can be intense. Please be transparent with yourself about your current state of being; this practice is meant to build resilience, and not to bond us more tightly with our binaried perception of Past trauma. Safety is key when initiating this type of deep meditative practice. It is best not to engage with the straight walk if states of exhaustion, or massive amounts of self-created and/or external stress are knocking at the door. If you find yourself in one of these depleted states, this text is filled with beautiful practices that can serve as more gentle alternatives. Come back to this walking meditation when you feel like you have greater access to your human and earthly resources.

Practicing this meditation in a quiet place is preferable. We want to create a sense of safety within the body/mind so the totality of the inner world can come to the surface.

Set your space as follows:
Stand at what we will call point "A." At point A, imagine a whole, radiant, and content version of self. Take several moments to pause here at this

initial starting location.

Begin to walk in a straight line towards what you have deemed point "B," about 20-25 steps ahead of you. At point B, place a version of self that you would like more clarity, depth, understanding, and realization around. This is generally an older version of self you feel limited by, in terms of Past choices, beliefs, relationships, and moments of extreme dis-ease that seem to affect your current perception of self.

Begin to walk away from point A and towards Point B. Feel ALL AND EVERY sensation that arises as you walk away from your "content version of self" to a "limited version of self." As you approach point B, stand still for a moment with your eyes closed. Imagine standing eye-to-eye with that old version of self. Feel its embodiment, and evoke the chemical state of the memories.

Slowly, and deliberately, take a half turn. Turn your back to that limited version of self.

Pause for several breaths with your back to point B. Experience a moment of deep release, grief, fear, excitement, empowerment, facing the unknown, letting go of the familiar. Pause here in the context of your memory and past version of self.

Slowly walk away from that mode of being you placed at point B, back towards the content version of you at point A. Pause facing point A and embody that vision in the chemical landscape of you.

Straight walk between these two points for at least 15 minutes per day during your 30-day work with this chapter.

Set your timer for three-minute intervals and keep a pen and paper close. You will straight walk for three minutes, and then sit and write, stream-of-consciousness, for three minutes. Try not to self-edit: write down each and every sensation, thought, and reaction you have during the process.

As you repeat the practice, you can play with engaging different versions of self. Let this be an organic process; work with a given Point B for as many consecutive straight walks as you need to redesign consciousness around these given junctures.

For example, there have been times I have worked with a limited version of myself at point B for months on end. In other practices, I have worked with limited versions of myself at point B that only required a few days of attention.

Keep your Expansive Listening Journal with you for this 30-day period as well. You are creating an out-road away from the limitations of your Associative Architecture and an in-road towards Clairsentience, breaking the Past/Future binary through your embodiment.

CLOSING WORDS

Dear one, this entire text—each section, and its words—holds a "threshold" frequency.

Step through, and you and the world around you will never be the same.

There are only a few times in this non-binary process that I speak from the identity of Sue Hunt.

I often don't lead with "personal experience" because I know my experiences are radically different from yours. Within the majority of this 9-month Consciousness Design Process, each binary is anthropomorphized through the eyes and experiences of many, which I've synthesized using my words.

I wanted to write these closing words directly from my heart to yours.

There will be times when your contemplations lead you to heavy, intensive, ego-shattering places. It will be difficult and radically freeing to hold this non-binary frequency in your heart, in your relationships, and in your communities.

I trust you, your strength, and your ability to rewire and hold this seat of deep love, appreciation, and openness for yourself and the world around you. Promise me that you will retire your soap box, and seek instead to live from your embodied Transitory Nature, beyond the binary. Even in the darkest corners of your mind. And especially when no one is watching.

No more preaching, or forceful teaching, or being "right" is necessary when we can embody multiple truths at once within our own hearts.

I needed this work—we all need this work—to live in the unique form it takes within you!

In complete integrity, I trust.

Thank you for engaging with the Consciousness Design Process, sharing your embodied inner changes with me, with loved ones, with friends, and with your extended communities.

The world will respond to your integrity and authenticity, and it will give others the space to radiate within their own.

From the blood, sweat, and tears that went into this work, I bow to your process.

Love,
Sue

tro
spects Differences
ids opposites w/o conflict
ndlessly Regenerative
xpands resilience of your central nervous system to
mbody creative solutions / enacts personal and
ocial change.

"Right choice" → small sliver of the full picture.

Energy exchange / Intrinsic Resources
Dis sexism...

Associative Architecture
Boundless Intimacy w/ our own self-identities
./ Public personna vs. deeply personal intimate
self
nchecked, unethical political systems continue to go
nchallenged
I Integrated personal messages / mind over body
Heirarchy / Trauma stored in auric fields or in
(or imprints)
electromatic frequency of entire body /mind.
cis-normative heteropatriarchy = bears subconscious
gender projections and energetic projections

ACKNOWLEDGEMENTS & ENDLESS APPRECIATION

To My Contributors.

Talia Migliaccio ~ Cover Art & Chapter Ink Mandalas

Becky Jane Krotts ~ Drawings & Mantra, Mudra, Subtle Body Sketches
Nicholas Graham ~ Moving Image & Digital Portals

Ruby Warrington & Bess Matassa ~ Visionaries & Editing Dream Team

To My Teachers.

Loving gratitude to my main Sanskrit teachers Raviji and Mayaji from Port of
Spain, Trinidad and Tobago. As well as time spent in Chennai, India in deep
study at Krishnamacharya Yoga Mandiram.

Richard Rosen, teacher, author and a no nonsense transmitter of truth for me
along the path for the last decade.

Paramatma Siri Sadhana, the embodiment of love and my open hearted guide
in ancient sikh teachings and astrology.

Swami Radha, no longer in her physical form. A radical force in shaping my
view of tantra and contextualizing the evolutionary core of ancient teachings.

Thank you for your authenticity and sharing transformational knowledge
with many.

To My Soulmate.

It's you who taught me about transcending polarity, and stepping into my
non-binary embodiment. Thank you for holding the space for me to create
this work.

Made in United States
Troutdale, OR
08/11/2023

11984932R00162